GW01417679

STRING QUARTET PLAYING

I. Fink & C. Merriell
with the
Guarneri String Quartet

Cover photo by Dorothea V. Haeften

ISBN 0-86622-007-0

Paganiniana Publications, Inc.
211 West Sylvania Avenue, Neptune City, N.J. 07753

This year, 1985, the Guarneri String Quartet celebrates its Twentieth Anniversary.

"On recalling and evaluating the many occasions I have enjoyed listening to the Guarneri, I suddenly realized that they have been doing the very things I have advocated for thirty years. I owe the inspiration for this book to the Guarneri Quartet, and it is with the greatest admiration and appreciation that I dedicate this work to them."

Irving Ilms

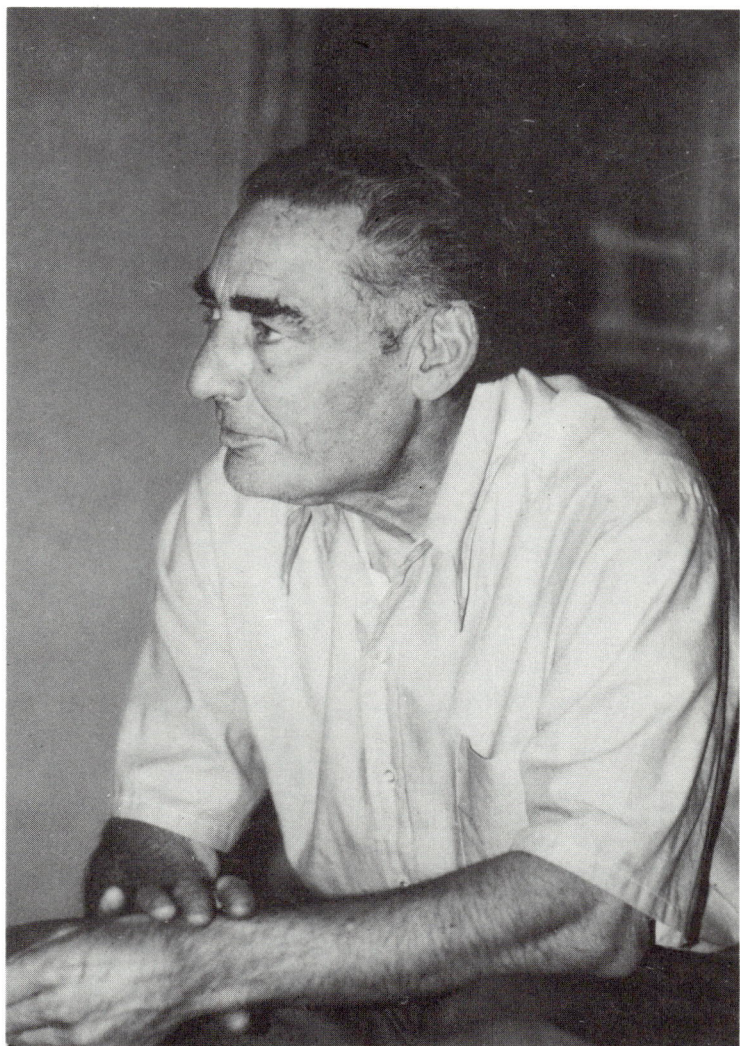

Red-line analysis (black in our publication) of a page in the Ravel Quartet.

Contents

The Guarneri Quartet, one of the finest in the world today.

Foreword

Comparison of ensembles large and small (from full orchestra to chamber ensembles in all their diversity) reveals the string quartet to be the ultimate form of musical communication – unmatched in conception and in performance.

There is a common misconception that the string quartet is a solo voice supported by two middle voices and a bass. This impression, based partly on the earlier music written for string ensembles and partly on the melody-oriented Western ear, has dominated the conception of the string quartet throughout history. If the violinists in such groups trade positions, it is almost invariably with the thought that one is taking the harder part while the other takes the easier. This view will be discussed further in the section which describes the functions of the instruments.

It is the author's intent to make very clear the distinction between this impression of the string quartet and what the string quartet *really* is conceptually, potentially, and as realized by ensembles of the finest caliber.

In describing the range of string quartet participation – from amateur to professional – it is hoped that this book will be of value to each reader, whatever his or her level of proficiency. There are references to the myriad techniques that can be employed, both to bring out the individual part and to add to the total luster of the ensemble.

The book will delve into the function of each instrument (with interviews with the members of the Guarneri Quartet accompanying each section), exploring how to play together to produce ensemble-sound, and examining six levels of tone-production.

String Quartet Playing presents the Red-Line System (explained later on) and dissects representative movements from three quartets—Mozart's "Dissonant," Beethoven's Op. 59, No. 2, and Ravel's—drawing attention in all the pertinent parts to those individualities, stresses, and balances that will produce the transcendent result of which, it seems, only the finest quartets are capable.

The author's preference for the string quartet over all other ensembles evolved gradually through his experience in, and observation of, virtually every possible combination of instruments. This preference, while not essential for everyone in string quartet participation, is what compelled him to gather his thoughts (and those of like-minded others) and to present them in this book.

The string quartet alone has the desired complex harmony with separate parts which span the whole range of tonality and individuality and which are matched for timbre. The four instruments fuse together into a perfectly balanced whole and the string quartet becomes a musical entity whose product is greater than the sum of its parts.

Needless to say, such a sublime ensemble is not a guaranteed result of just any four people deciding to tackle, say, a Beethoven quartet. Although some of the finest compositions have been written for the string quartet, a great deal besides technical proficiency is required from the players.

String Quartet Playing very much advocates working with a score, as it is essential for each player to have a sense of the whole. This brings us to the reason those four players have gotten together in the first place: the music.

Almost every composer has tried his hand at writing string quartets because he regarded the form as the ideal of a balanced ensemble to produce works capable of every nuance, every subtlety, every possibility of tone color (exceeded in that only by a full symphony orchestra), while at the same time honing the ensemble so that a fine quartet actually sounds like a single instrument, yet is capable of infinitely more possibilities, in certain respects, than any other combination of instruments.

The very fact that a string quartet is the apogee of ensemble playing and has a clarity that projects the composer's inmost thoughts, at the same time makes a quartet much more difficult to conceive, arrange and present. Every phrase in a string quartet must have musical meaning and must contribute to the message of the work as a whole. With the quartet, as an ensemble, being so small and limited, there is no way of covering up any weak spots in the musical thoughts of the composer. In a quartet, all is clarity; nothing can be hidden. Here we have a vehicle where we deal with what one might call the bare bones of music. It is the sheer inspiration, lucidity, and craftsmanship of the composer that must carry the music.

Later on, one of our axioms will be that whenever there is a "dead" spot in the music, it is not the composer's fault. Somebody is not stressing or playing his or her part, because the composer of a fine string quartet never lets a measure lie dormant. Every measure has its full quota of musical thoughts, well-organized and, in the finer quartets, divinely inspired. In a fine quartet you will not find any filler.

The perfectly balanced ensemble is able to achieve such a unanimity of spirit that the four instruments form a single whole which, in itself, becomes an entirely new and different instrument. New vistas of musical thought are opened to listeners, and the music enters an enchanted realm which may truly be called transcendental.

The Guarneri Quartet on the move.

THE FUNCTION OF EACH INSTRUMENT

That you are reading this book means that you are not only a quartet devotee, but probably a string player who indulges in the extraordinary art of string quartet playing, with perhaps varying degrees of success. You know that the skills and levels of mastery, the personalities present, the chamber music experience each player has had, the rapport attainable in the immediate group, are all factors which affect the success of the ensemble. You have probably discovered that, even in the beginning stages of the average amateur group, it is likely that at least one of those present will have definite ideas of direction for the quartet: the composer, the degree of difficulty to be tackled, tempi, even the manner of interpretation.

It is essential that any group, from the most enthusiastic amateurs to the skilled professionals, have direction and goals if it is going to try to bring to life even a facsimile of the composer's creation. There is a need for leadership in all quartets. In an amateur group, however, that need tends to result in a hierarchy within the quartet. The casual quartet — feeling the need for leadership and being subject to a natural amount of inertia — usually relies on the first violin for security. Indeed, the structure of early string quartet music (with the first violin carrying the major melodic and technical load; the second violin in a literally secondary, less demanding position; the viola a subordinate, middle voice; the cello a supporting bass) strengthens the tendency for quartets to defer to the first violin.

David Soyer, cellist of the Guarneri Quartet.

Each instrument holds a unique and essential position within the ensemble and has its own special function to perform in all quartet music, from early through modern. But the exciting truth—even in the early music and increasingly in the later compositions and in modern music—is that *each* instrument must, at various times, take the *lead* and *set* the style, the pace, even the mood of the moment. At such times that instrument *must* take the leading role while the others must sublimate and match *whatever* the lead is doing. Each player has to be ever alert, acutely aware and responsive, supporting and sometimes leading! The string quartet is a most demanding form in which to participate. There is absolutely *no* room for deadwood—either in performers or in performance. There is never an excuse—not even in the early Haydn, the young Mozart, or the most obscure of a composer's works—to lapse into a "let George do it" level of participation.

You are vital—whatever your instrument—to the quartet. Before you set bow to string, you must be mentally prepared to bring the work to *life*. With alert sensitivity to what your part is saying, to what each of the other voices is doing, to what the leader of the moment is inviting you to match, you will lift your performance to a higher level, and in so doing fulfill the incredible potential the string quartet has of transcending the sum of its parts.

Now let's explore the special function of each instrument. The description of each role played in a quartet will be followed by an interview with the member of the Guarneri Quartet who plays that role.

THE CELLO

The strength of the cello in the quartet does not lie in its obvious size and inherent capacity for volume (although that can be utilized most effectively). The cello is the tonal foundation of the quartet. One of its primary roles is that, being able to produce the lowest bass tones of the ensemble,

A good quartet always pays attention to what the viola has to say.

it gives the greatest possible contrast to the soprano range of the violins. Its potential is most effectively revealed (as is so with each of the instruments) through the judicious and artistic use of tone colors and dynamic emphasis. As one of the four ensemble soloists, the cellist must not only act as the tonal bass of the quartet, but must be able to furnish the highest level of solo tone quality. Again, this does not mean volume. Solo type of tone quality while playing softly is one of the most important aspects of quartet playing.

This point calls to mind an occasion when a private quartet, among whose members was a very fine cellist, was playing a Brahms quartet. The top three strings were going along, à la typical Brahms — counter melodies, counter surges, all kinds of passion back and forth. The cello had the most beautiful counter melody of all, but was playing along very calmly. Finally, the cellist was urged, "You've got such beautiful counter melodies in there. Bring them out! Play. Let it go. Give more. When a cellist gets hold of something as beautiful as that phrase, you can't hold him down! He gives it all he's got!" The cellist's response was, "But it's marked *piano!*"

This kind of reasoning, as applied to the string quartet, is a million miles off the mark. Almost every quartet has been edited half a dozen times. Every editor, for one reason or another, has changed dynamics and otherwise altered the music. We also have the practical fact that the poor composer (because he is so pressed for time, or is disgusted, or for a thousand other reasons) just is not going to mark the four parts, "One play *mezzo piano*, the next one *mezzo forte*; one play *solo piano* and the other play *solo forte*." He simply puts down *mezzo piano* for all four parts. In his mind he hears the way he'd like to hear it played. It is up to the performers to interpret the intentions of the composer, so as to bring out the spirit of the music and actualize its full potential. While that interpretation may be in the style of the particular group, one of the wonderful things about music is

18

that each performance is, in a way, a recreation of the music. There really is no hard and fast rule as to exactly how the music should be played, whether it be rhythm, dynamics, quality of tone, harmonies, tempo, or anything else. What the composer has set down is an indication of what he thinks the music should be like. The rest is up to the performer. It is the performer's interjection of varying emphases that is the essence of great playing.

The Brahms performance mentioned above was clearly the time for the cellist to let loose with a glorious *solo obbligato* tone. The fact that it was marked *piano* was not vital. That does not mean the part must be brought out *forte*. What it does mean is that here we want absolute solo quality: a solo tone, full *vibrato*, big bows, take charge. This is just the time not to hide one's light under a bushel!

The cellist is usually the one responsible for the bottom range of tone production, which, in most cases, involves rhythmic stability as well as the playing of whole notes. It is deadly to fine quartet playing to have an instrument simply draw notes. Each note should be vibrated and fitted in with what is going on with the rest of the quartet. Sometimes, on a particular note, a quick *vibrato* will emphasize that there's been a harmonic change or a new melody has started. The point is, there is no such thing as a static note that just hangs on. Things are happening all the time, and that long note can be just as important as any other part. Furthermore, in the overall beauty of production in the quartet, we have all heard how a master cellist can let that single tone dramatize and vitalize the entire musical tapestry.

Interview with David Soyer, Cellist

What would you consider the role of the cellist in quartet playing?

Basically, in the classic repertoire you think of it as the bass of the harmonic structure. Then, you also think of it as the base of the quartet, in the sense that the acoustic foundation is created by the cello. It's a kind of platform, hopefully a big, wide one, for the other instruments to rest on.

The cello is actually the instrument that has probably the greatest range of the three instruments—in having a five octave range which, in the repertoire through the 20th century, is actually used. You do find it in Mozart, and Beethoven. When you start getting into the later Romantic works—Ravel, Bartók—you find that a tremendous compass is used in the cello. Five octaves! I think violins usually use not more than three, three-and-a-half octaves. As a result, the cello actually takes on many roles. Aside from the classic one of the bass instrument, it's a tenor, alto or soprano on certain occasions, and then the roles of the other instruments switch. So you can't really say that it's a static thing—that the cello plays this role and the viola that one, etc., etc. It does change, depending on the music.

Speaking strictly of the Guarneri, what would you consider your particular role in the Guarneri Quartet? That is, since there are special circumstances—the caliber of the players you are with is so high—is there any difference in the way you consider your performance with the Guarneri?

Well, just what I've said before: the instrumental part itself would always serve those same functions. In the Guarneri Quartet? Basically, there's no great difference . . . perhaps the fact that we're four very strong players may create a greater difference, perhaps, in the playing than you might find in other groups where you may have one weak link or two weak links.

Well, for instance, might you rely more on their skill and take, say, more chances . . . a sudden *pianissimo* ?

Oh, that, now I understand what you mean. Yes, that may be the case, yes . . . that's very possible. Yes, in a way we're free . . . freer of instrumental strictures.

Now, how do you consider that you maintain your so-called "perfect ensemble" in the Guarneri? By what means do you achieve this terrifically high ensemble level?

David Soyer, cellist.

Well, there's . . . perhaps it's a philosophy . . . What we're attempting to do, really, is to play together, and *not* follow. And there *is* a difference. There have been excellent quartets in the past where the three other players follow the first fiddler, and do it very skillfully. But the impetus all comes from that one instrument, and you have a very subtle sort of secondary lagging feeling . . . not in actuality, but in feeling. They may be perfectly well together, but there's a certain energy lacking in the ensemble. And our attempt is that we all four sort of look for . . . all try to play to a central point, and we all go for that, together, rather than one of us doing and the others quickly taking up that lead.

The difference in sound is that there's a greater vitality. When it succeeds, it's very successful. When it fails, it's a much greater disaster. So, it's chancier, in a sense, but it still is well worth the risk. When something goes awry, it's a complete catastrophe. But, if it's together, it's really together, and one feels it.

Do you, personally, like all the music you play? For instance, the Lutoslawski or some other abstract modern work. Do you really like every bit of music you play? Is there a difference of opinion or do you arrive at a consensus? How do you arrive at what you're going to play?

Obviously, being four individuals, everyone has a subjective reaction to a particular piece of music. Of the Beethoven Quartets, I might like one particularly; the others may prefer another. If you say, "Which is your favorite Beethoven quartet?" you may have four different quartets given, and, as I say, that's a subjective reaction. We only play music we like; we don't play music we don't like, because we don't feel we *can*. We really can't *do* anything with music we don't like and, therefore, we won't play it. In a quite modern piece like the Lutoslawski, again the reactions are subjective. I think probably some of us like it more than others. We all admire it, we all think it's good or we wouldn't be playing it. If, for example, three say, "Oh, let's play that piece. It's terrific!" and the other one says, "I hate it!" we don't play it. Can't be done. We disagree sometimes on the extent of how good the work is. This Lutoslawski quartet, for example . . . if you asked all of us about it, individually, you'd probably get four somewhat different answers. I think, for example, that Arnold and I like it less than John and Michael, though still, we *do* like it. It's that . . . you know . . . it's a question of degree. But, as I say, as far as the standard repertoire's concerned, one could hardly argue with Opus 131, or something like that, and say, "I don't like that piece."

I noticed in last night's program you played a Schubert which, incidentally, I had never heard before.

Yes, the little one in B flat major . . . beautiful.

How did you come to select that, for instance . . . just searching for new repertoire?

Well, you know, we set up programs every season, and it was a question of balance. We needed a rather light work of that period. As I remember it, one of us had heard a recording of the piece, of some group playing, and was rather struck by it as a nice work. And then we said, "Let's look at it and see what we think," and we chose it. I find it a charming and beautiful piece. At first, I expected that perhaps it wouldn't "wear." I mean the cello part. To play the cello part . . . you know . . . it's not so challenging instrumentally, nor are any of the other parts but the first fiddle, really, though there are little tunes here and there. But it's so fresh and so delightful. I really do enjoy the piece very much.

How closely do you follow each other's execution? For instance, do you attempt to imitate the other players' bowings or they imitate yours . . . things of that sort . . . dynamics, phrasings . . . what is your philosophy in that direction?

Well, that would very much depend on the musical context. We don't make a big point of each one sounding alike. As a matter of fact, we don't really think that's a terribly good idea. We do it when we feel that it serves the piece. If a phrase is immediately repeated by another instrument, for example, and it seems to need an exact copy of its predecessor, then we do that. That's part of musical choice. As I say, we don't make a point.

In fact, sometimes we think it's desirable that each voice has its own individual quality, that the melody played by the viola shouldn't necessarily sound the same way as that just having been played by the fiddle. It is a different instrument, has a different timbre and a different quality in the fact that the composer has chosen to voice the piece by using the first violin playing a melody followed by the viola playing it. He's chosen the viola because of the timbre. He wants a quality . . . a certain texture . . . a certain character . . . which sound the viola has, as opposed to giving it to the second fiddle, perhaps, which would be playing in the same range. But he wants that sound. Or giving it to the cello, perhaps, who also could possibly be playing in the same range as the viola just played it, or the second fiddle, or the first, or whatever the case may be. It's a different character. So we feel, in the end, the individual player has latitude to play the tune his way, unless it's completely out of the question, of course. Then we confer on that.

The philosophy is to actually stress the different characteristics and the different timbres of the various instruments?

Yes. Of course, I mean the player of the different instrument, either the viola or the cello in this case, would have a different approach to playing. It's a different kind of thing, but we . . . we find that desirable. The fact is that we're four very distinct personalities, as players, and *that* in itself we use, really . . . perhaps not so terribly consciously, but we do use it.

Is the quartet always in top form? Or is there a special inspiration arising from the auditorium, or the climate, or the circumstances under which you play?

Let's say I think we're always in top form. Yes, we never play below a certain level. From the negative side, if we're very tired or in a situation where there's not much feedback from the audience, for example (which is a very important part of the concert), you may get less excitement or spontaneity or vitality in the performance. But, we always try. We're always trying to play as well as we possibly can. And we play so many performances. In a hundred performances, you're bound to have some better than others or worse than others.

Actually, I was pointing to the question of whether there ever arises what one might call a magical evening where everything falls into place?

Certainly, yes, that does happen. What creates it is hard to know. It might be a big occasion, an especially exciting event, a Carnegie Hall performance, or what have you, in a very important music center with a great, huge audience. Sometimes it's not that. It may sometimes be just one of those nights, you know, some special situation where it clicks—bang—and goes on from there . . . because we have played sometimes especially good concerts in rather small, obscure places.

That concludes my questions. Are there any other observations you'd like to make?

Well, just to amplify the thing about differences among the players . . . kind of an interesting analogy would be: you take your fiddle, cello, or viola, and you have a choice of a fingering. You can play on the A string and you can play the same notes on the D string, and you choose to play them on the D string. Why? Because of the timbre. You want a color; you want a specific kind of sound. You don't want to have it sound exactly the way it sounds on the A string. You want some difference. That would be a comparable thing. It's also kind of amusing that people take an instrument and say, "Gee, it's terrifically even—every string; one string sounds exactly like the other!" which I would think wouldn't be too desirable. What the hell's the difference? Why have four different strings if they're all going to sound alike? Have one great long one, and play everything on one string! I know that my students . . . most of my students (and most cellists, now) play, for example, with a steel A and a steel D, and I say to the kids, "But, why do you want the steel D string?" (I don't like them. They're very rigid and they're a little bit reedy sounding and the fifths are never good.) And they say, "Well, 'cause it matches the A . . . sounds the *same* as the A string." And I say, "Why do you want it to sound the same as the A string? It's *not* the A string, it's the D string. What's the big deal?" Or, by the same token, if frogs' legs taste like chicken, you know, why not eat chicken, and why bother with frogs' legs? Same thing. And, in a way, I mean, that's the kind of thing in following one phrase after another.

That is a very interesting concept. In other words, instead of striving to make one instrument sound like another, you *accentuate* the differences? An arresting concept, indeed!

And as I say, it's a musical concept. If it's desired in a particular piece that the one line goes very smoothly without a seam and sounds just the same, so that you have a long descending passage of one instrument after another, then, fine, we certainly do attempt to play as much alike as possible, bowings included. As for bowings, we'll play the same ones if it's necessary. Sometimes we won't. Sometimes people are kind of bemused by the fact that they look at Arnold and John playing the same passage, and one is going up and one is going down, and they think they must be arguing or fighting. If you can make the same sound in a phrase and with two different bowings, fine. What's the difference? Maybe one of us is more comfortable with one than the other. If it's necessary that our strokes be absolutely alike, then very often we *do* make the same bowings. We do phrasing the same way, if it's a question of phrasing, or what have you, but there is no basic rule such as, "Yes, everybody plays down bow at the same time, etc."

I would like to have you expand a little more on "dynamic range." You didn't say much about that. The impression I got is that in a big auditorium such as you usually play in, you don't really let it get down to triple *pianissimo*. You reserve enough to carry out. Is that deliberate?

I think that's a question of experience. When you're always involved in the projection of an idea, one begins to "feel" at what point it's too soft or too loud, whatever the case may be, and again it's a musical judgment; it's a musical choice. It is true we do not play in a miniature fashion.

Even in a small room, for instance?

No, we don't make any attempt to change. It's too difficult to do that. We never try a hall before a concert, even if it's a place we've never been in before, because we find it's really pointless. If it's good, it's good. And if it's no good, there's nothing you can do about it. You can't make it better. And the acoustics . . . we adjust; you know . . . a few notes and we know right away what sort of sound it is, and we adjust to that. But we don't change the playing to suit the hall.

Now, when you mentioned the base of the quartet, does that also imply rhythmic energy or control? The cellist would be the leader of that type of thing?

Yes, of course. Rhythmic . . . energy or emphasis; yes, in some situations. Again, it's not a static thing. It may be changed. The viola might do it, but, generally the cello would be giving the figures of the bass in a steady fashion. Sometimes a change of harmony or the bass note or the way the bass note is changed can affect the way the chord sounds or the way it gives the players impetus.

I'd like to focus more specifically. In listening to your ensemble play, the cello seems to be the major factor in getting a thing started or keeping it going because of its greater strength in every direction.

You're talking about rhythmic impetus?

Rhythmic . . . almost every direction . . . certainly in

rhythm, when the cello starts out a phrase, it sets the rhythm in the strongest sense. It's just natural.

If the music is structured that way and the tempo, yes, the tempo's in the hands of the cello. That sometimes is the case.

In that sense, it's stronger than the other instruments, naturally, but also you make a point of it.

Yes, well . . . I don't mean to put myself up, but we're very strong, all of us, and we insist on our own functions very strongly, and we carry them out very strongly. All four. So it may seem, compared perhaps to some other ensembles, that you've noticed this—I don't know how to put it—this strength, if you want, of the cello part.

There's no hesitancy.

Hopefully not!

No. That's one of the earmarks of your ensemble's playing.

Yes, well, that's our way of playing.

It makes a tremendous effect.

Yes, I think that may be so. You know, I can think of other groups where that's a weak spot. But, that's a fault, of course. It's not that *ours* is a plus; *theirs* is a fault.

Well, the reason I asked the question this way was as a pointer . . . that the cello, especially the cello, should never be hesitant.

No, certainly not.

Nor any of the other instruments, but the cello especially.

Yes, right! It's, again, the same thing. Everybody going toward the same point, in the center. It's the same philosophy because everybody's trying to make one out of four. And that's really what it is. So not one person is hesitant . . . following only sometimes, only when necessary. If the musician's on his own, in a way, he's playing a tune, and we don't know . . . we won't know until he plays it . . . just exactly what he's going to do. Because we do give ourselves— each other—that leeway. I mean, we never set "rubati."

I have one final question. There has been some discussion exchanged with members of your group that in certain instances, or in general, you do a minimum of head nodding and leading. You've almost reached a level of . . . we might call it ESP. What is your view on this type of ensemble? What levels do you maintain most of the time? Do you get to a higher, mystical level?

Well, "mystical" may be not quite the right word. There are just certain things . . . we know each other's playing very well; we've been in all sorts of playing circumstances. We've played so much repertoire so many times in so many places under so many conditions. For instance, I know pretty well that when Arnold plays that melody, he's going to do "X" number of things. He's gonna slow down here or get faster there or be louder or softer . . . any number. There may be any six or seven permutations. But, I'm aware of that, and I'm not surprised by any of them. Generally not. Sometimes, yes, but generally not. We can anticipate each other's vagaries, perhaps, readily, from experience, and without having to have signals and pre-arranged ritards and what have you. I mean, we're aware . . . and, of course, that's the whole essence of chamber music playing, really . . . it's reactive.

Then, what would your advice be to the players on a less experienced level who don't get the chance to play a quartet 50 times?

Keep your ears open. It really is a question of listening and sensitivity. I know that in studying for quartet playing, a very valuable experience for me, as a cellist — a terrifically valuable experience — was playing a lot of *continuo* in Baroque music. I used to do a great deal of that. We really played a lot of it. Years ago Ralph Kirkpatrick, a harpsichordist, and I were a *continuo* team, and we used to play all the Bach works . . . the B minor . . . Mass. We used to play the B minor Mass and the St. Matthew and St. John Passions . . . and cantatas, and I was always playing bass. I was the *continuo*. *Chunk, chunk, wah, wah,* all the time for hours of it and with singers, and it was tremendously valuable.

Michael Tree, violist of the Guarneri Quartet.

We'd be learning, because you'd learn bass functions and follow and be flexible and all of this stuff . . . *recitative* playing . . . and all of these kinds of improvisatory things, and that was tremendous for me.

THE VIOLA

Now we come to the most interesting instrument in the entire ensemble, the viola. The viola is an instrument that can not only blend beautifully with the tones of the cello, but also equally well with both violins. It can reinforce melodies in all harmonic and tonal dimensions. Finally, the viola adds another ingredient which, by itself, is the most fascinating of all—the viola tone is completely different from and contrasts with that of the cello or the violin. One of the most fascinating effects in string quartet playing is achieved when the nasality of the viola A-string tone is emphasized and, especially, when it is used for contrast, whether in classical or modern music.

The entire range of the viola is unique. It doesn't sound like a cello or a violin; thus it can be used for all kinds of tonal effects. It covers the tenor range of the string quartet tonal spectrum and, as such, fulfills that most important part in the complete tonality. Harmonically, it is equally interesting, because, usually, as chords and harmony become more and more sophisticated, the leading tones are increasingly performed by the viola. It is much easier for an instrument with this unique tone to bring out the leading edge of the various harmonic modulations.

The viola has an interesting history. In early chamber music and early quartets, the viola was simply an instrument to fill the tenor part of the composition. As we get to the later Haydn, the great Mozart, the incomparable Beethoven quartets, the viola is called on more and more to stress leading tones, to furnish contrasting melodies and, in later compositions, to become the instrument that is used like an unusual color in an impressionistic painting. For these reasons the viola is capable of tonal effects that are unique. The viola, then, is the most fascinating instrument in the entire ensemble. It has a tonal range as great as that of any of the other instruments, the capability of producing many more qualities of tone, and a uniqueness that no other instrument in the ensemble can match—from the nasality of the A string through the whole rich amber to opalescent spectrum of viola tone color. For example, we can go back to our old standby, the Ravel Quartet, and listen to what can be done with the viola part. It's absolutely like an Impressionist painter putting in the strangest colors just when you least expect it, yet somehow bringing out the piquancy of the painting so that one has an entirely fresh outlook, or impression, of the composition. With the Ravel, after the initial theme, the second violin and viola come in with a background that is tonally entirely new; it contains tone colors never before projected. Sometimes the strange background becomes the theme, and the original theme becomes *obbligato*. There is a new *pizzicato*—suggesting harps, guitar, and other percussive effects in a new manner.

This brings up another aspect of the role of the viola—the unexpectedness of the viola's quality of tone. In many, many compositions of all types, from strictly classical to extreme modern, the viola will come in with a contrasting timbre and add a piquancy to the sound that is most effective and is one of the most attractive of string quartet capabilities.

Interview with Michael Tree, Violist

What would you say is the special role of the viola in a string quartet, or, especially, how would you define your role in the Guarneri Quartet, Mr. Tree?

First of all, I think all of the instruments in a quartet, being so finely integrated and so crucial, enjoy an equal role. Certainly the role of any given instrument depends on exactly what's happening at the moment within the music. There are moments when any of the instruments will play

Michael Tree, violist.

either a predominant lead voice or a so-called accompaniment. I say "so-called" because I think that's a misnomer. Any accompaniment figure that sounds like an accompaniment is already bound to hurt the group. A "supportive role," perhaps, would be the more correct term, even when the viola plays a secondary voice as, say, in a classic work of Mozart or early Beethoven when there's a typical kind of eighth-note or sixteenth-note accompaniment figure. That has to enhance the lead voice or the melodic line at that moment and even inspire it to go further or to play better. And, of course, that also shifts from moment to moment.

I'd say the only unique role that the viola ever plays in a quartet ·that the others, of course, can't—is that it does occupy a rather pivotal position tonally in the quartet. At moments, it lends itself more to the soprano quality of the upper strings. Then it also is used in almost a duet sense with the cello. And sometimes, when the cello plays a melody, the viola then becomes the bass of the quartet, and we have to learn from the cello, then, how to play kind of a figured bass figure, or provide a floor or bottom to the quartet. So, it (the viola) does all these things, and it's interesting to note that when Mozart and Schubert and Beethoven played string quartets at home, they usually chose to play the viola, perhaps because sitting in the middle of the group they got a better insight and a better overall, almost "stereo" appreciation of what was going on around them.

How do you maintain the so-called perfect ensemble in your group? Is there some special formula you follow, or just what is it that you do to achieve this perfect ensemble?

I have to thank you for the word "perfect," Irv. It's far from that. We work very hard in keeping our tools sharpened. We don't ever allow too many concerts to go by—even on tour, in the midst of a hectic season—without sitting down and reminding ourselves, over and over again, that there are places that are never quite together, or that there are differences in the attack of certain passages in the inner voices. There's a lot of difficult ensemble work that has to be quite . . . I wouldn't use the word "perfect," but . . . it has to be well together, and there is no short cut to that. We have to agree on certain basic principles in bowing, and then we have to just keep working at it. And if we find that we're slipping a little bit . . . sometimes constant playing, under concert conditions, is not always very good for our technique (you've played in orchestras, so you know what happens if you constantly play and don't rehearse or practice), and then the playing tends to become a little sloppy or dirty.

What you said about the inner voices being particularly intermeshed is very interesting. Can you go a little bit further into the importance of their meshing together and supplying a solid background or a very clear background?

Well, maybe we give more importance to the inner voices than other groups have in the past. I consider, for example, that the second violin part—which also is, of course, a misnomer—is more crucial, in terms of overall ensemble, than anyone. Again, in the classic literature—when the upper voice, or the melodic line, has a long melody to play— it's the second violinist who really keeps the ensemble tight. He almost serves as a conductor while the upper voice or the melodic line, is playing, more or less, freely. And that's very crucial. I find myself looking diagonally across the quartet at John more often than at anyone else. Because, if I feel at one with him, then I feel both of us can move as one instrument in complementing whatever is happening in either the cello or the first violin part. Of course, that's in accompaniment-type playing.

Do you like every piece that you perform? I was just thinking of the Lutoslawski composition you played recently. Are there various opinions or do you arrive at a consensus? How do you arrive at the performance of the pieces that you do, especially the modern ones?

Well, Irv, as you can imagine, in any democracy there is a

lot more discussion and argument than one might think. As far as repertoire is concerned, we certainly don't agree on what we would like to live with for a season, because when we choose a work it has to be over the long haul—it has to be something that we're willing to play perhaps 50 or 60 times in a year—and that's a lot different from choosing a work simply to be played occasionally or for sheer pleasure's sake. We just thrash it out. And I'm the one who's personally responsible for programming. Of course, I can't act unilaterally, but I have to kind of put together programs assuming the others know more or less what's going on. Sometimes, when exceptions have to be made or when works for one reason or another are not acceptable to the local auspices, we have to invent new programs. For example, tomorrow night we're playing a Haydn quartet here that we're not traveling with at all this year. I had to decide upon that, because they didn't want any Beethoven quartets. The reason was that last year we had played the entire cycle here. *That* I had to decide on my own, but I knew that we had traveled with that piece a year ago and it wouldn't be too hard for us to bring it back. Otherwise, I must say that we never play music that we don't like. It just may happen that some of us like some music more than the others, and we've had good healthy disagreements about that.

Now, there's a question about the ensemble's control of the dynamic range. How do you control the dynamic range or the complete range of your playing? Do you determine it beforehand, or is it led by the leader, or is a certain way of playing set when the quartet is started and then carried all the way through?

A little bit of everything. First of all, naturally we try and obey the composer's markings, but that leaves a lot of further leeway, and composers couldn't be expected to phrase for us—they can't make ups and downs and *diminuendi* and *crescendi* and fade outs and *subito* changes in dynamics. We often have to improve on the composer's markings. All of this is carefully rehearsed, and then there is always that element of improvisation that should happen every night, and differently each time. And that happens through experience, I guess. If we feel that a lead voice at the moment is in danger of being covered, then it's up to everyone to get out of his way and allow him enough latitude to do something unexpected. To make a sudden phrasing or a sudden diminuendo—the sort of thing that an actor might do on the spur of the moment—,to that we all have to immediately respond.

How closely do you follow each other's execution? In this case I'm referring to the idea that if the leader has one style of bowing, does everyone else try to do the same downs and ups and *spiccatos?* Do they try to follow his styles? Or, just *how* do you go about this problem of uniform bowings and fingerings and phrasings?

It depends very much, Irv, on the writing. If it's in a so-called "concerted" passage when two or more instruments have to sound like one (for example, in octaves or thirds or sixths, or whatever), then we do try and bow alike, or somewhat alike, but even so we're not at all dogmatic about it. I think other groups have made a much bigger thing of sounding like one homogeneous group. We don't attempt that, often. As a matter of fact, we think there's something quite interesting about a melody being tossed from one person to another and not sounding quite alike.

And yet you achieve a remarkable sonority of tone, and in this business of transcending the limitations of each individual instrument and coming out with a single tone of the ensemble—to my mind, you do it better than anybody else. To what do you attribute this result?

I don't know, Irv, except to say that we realize now that everybody has a preferred way of doing anything, and if somebody happens to be a little happier at the tip or at the frog or on the A string or on the D string or playing up-bow or down-bow, we let it happen. We only attempt to arrive at a uniform *sound* but not a technically uniform way of playing. In other words, we don't insist on everybody playing together and doing everything at the same time. Even in *spiccato* work (and I would use for an example the Op. 59, No. 1, the slow movement, which has a lot of off-the-string work), some of us are much happier playing up, up, up. I prefer it because I get a little more air between the notes, and more crispness and more control. But then others prefer doing down, up, down, up. Now if the difference in sound is apparent, then we have to come to some sort of understanding about it. But, if the difference is not apparent, then often we'll contradict each other onstage and play the way we like.

I have a feeling that last statement will be very interesting to our Saturday-night groups.

Maybe a little troubling!

Now for my last question. Do you consider yourselves to always be in top form, or can outside influences occur that cause some kind of inspirational concert, some event—maybe playing in Carnegie Hall? Just how do you regard your various performances when it comes to maintaining these technical or inspirational levels?

That's a tough one. I suppose there are unconscious influences. We try never to approach one concert any differently from another. Wherever we are, whether in a large hall or small, or whatever the program, we try not to play differently, or in any way to be influenced by our external surroundings. However, we know that's impossible. So, without our wanting to, I'm afraid we're all subject to the same uncertainties, or the same fatigues or problems that beset any performer. Travel is very exhausting and, often, having just gotten off an airplane, we are exhausted. I know that athletes complain about that, and they have strict rules regarding the amount of work or play they can do after long trips. We don't always have it as good as that, and sometimes there are accidents that occur. We find ourselves sitting in airports half a day and then running into the hall in our street clothes and having to play.

Is there anything you'd like to add, maybe some overall generalizations or observations about the quartet's performance as a whole?

There's a lot to talk about. It's a subject that's literally endless. Much of it enters almost into the intangible, the mystical side, because there is an element, somehow, of telepathy or something extramusical going on. That's hard to define and maybe even shouldn't be discussed. These things can only be experienced, I suppose, when technical considerations are put aside, and when you're at least fairly comfortable making music onstage and not self-conscious. But, there are great moments that are, to a musician, unforgettable. And we're lucky to have a repertoire that's endless. We can choose from any number of great works. We feel we haven't solved even half the repertoire that's available to us. We play the great works—all of the Beethoven and Mozart quartets, although not all of the young, very early Mozart quartets. Schubert wrote quartets that we don't know. The other night we played the E flat which is the first one he wrote, but there are probably a half dozen more like that, that we haven't played.

Is there any particular passage in the quartet repertoire that is expecially crucial for you as the viola? For example, in Op. 59, No. 3, the last movement.

Oh, there are many. The funny thing is that, except for the obvious moments, like the Smetana "Aus Mein Leben" or the opening of the Fugue of Op. 59, No. 3, there are hundreds of places where the viola is crucial and the writing is very difficult, but it's not generally known. Take the opening of the Brahms A minor quartet—all of that triplet writing. It's more or less out of the way. It's not meant to be heard in itself, or certainly above the other instruments, but it's very, very difficult and makes a perfect study for stringcrossing and would be just as good as any exercise written for the sake of achieving *legato*. One must be very fluid and yet able to adjust instantly to any deviations that might come in the rhythm around one. I was talking to a composer friend of mine the other day about a recording he had heard and told me about—I think Opus 131 of Beethoven played by string orchestra—and he asked me, as a quartet player, what I thought. I had to say that in that particular work, as in the case of the Big Fugue of Beethoven (which is also sometimes played by string orchestra) and in other works like the beautiful sextet of Tchaikovsky, which I also heard recorded with a full string orchestra, I think the idea is dreadful. It's a bad way of taking what is essentially chamber music and making it sound glossy and glib and soupy. My theory is that: an old teacher of mine—Tabuteau, who was the great oboe player and a great inspiration to all of us at Curtis—used to talk about the single razor blade being sharp. But the moment you add a second blade to it, it becomes a little less sharp; the cutting edge is reduced. If you add a third and fourth and fifth and sixth razor blade and stand them all up on end, you suddenly find yourself with a rather blunt instrument. The analogy is that in quartet playing, everyone is responsible, not only to himself, but to each other, and that every single note is crucial. A single misplaced note anywhere, even in the so-called "accompaniment figures," is instantly heard, and that puts a burden on us (a very beautiful burden) of playing well at every moment, not only for technical reasons, but, more importantly, to be musically inspired and involved all the time. We constantly have to play over our heads. The point I'm making is that when this music is played by too many people, the end result is too smooth, too effortless, too easy. And I can tell you that to play the "Big Fugue," the "Grosse Fuge" of Beethoven, is a struggle. It is a confrontation every night, and, believe me, you walk off the stage exhausted. Well, I think I could play that piece in an orchestra, under the greatest of conductors, probably a hundred times, with less energy than it takes to play the piece *once* for quartet. But I suspect Beethoven knew what he was doing. And I suspect that part of that struggle is intended.

I was thinking about the opening of the A minor Brahms. You take the theme for granted—everybody knows what the theme is—but the thing that always catches my attention is the accompaniment figure: it sounds like a solo.

It is ingenious counterpoint, and it would be unthinkable that the melody be played any other way.

What I really caught is that, when you do that viola part, it sounds like three instruments playing, alternating, you know, like a Schubert accompaniment might be broken up over several instruments. In fact, you're doing all the work; you're carrying the whole thing.

It's a very busy piece; almost turgid, at moments. I suppose it might sound a bit muddy or . . .

. . . Confusing, yes, and then it sort of thins out and you get the very beautiful . . .

. . . Yes, in the slow movement, sometimes, I have the feeling I'm wallowing in chocolate. It's so sensuous, and so rich, and the sounds are very, very flattering to a quartet. In some of the earlier music, it may be of interest to note that when we began recording the Beethoven quartets, we started with the late quartets, because we felt those were the easiest to play. The middle quartets came second. But then the early, the Opus 18 quartets, we wouldn't touch until we had played them many times in public, because they are the hardest.

What's so difficult about them?

Just that lack of sensuousness . . . that lack of sound or the enveloping . . . it's a naked feeling.

You know the reaction that I had? On hearing the cycle, the Opus 18's sounded harder than the 131's, and it was like a slap in the face. What is this? Twelve-year-olds play the Opus 18's, and we're afraid to touch the Opus 131's until we're 35 years old.

Obviously the intellectual content and the development,

the sense of style, especially in the late Beethoven quartets is unparalleled. He sidestepped the entire 19th Century in some of those works. Nevertheless, when we play an Opus 18 quartet, I feel that the concert is over for me. The rest of the concert just plays by itself, whether it's Ravel or Bartók, Hindemith or Schoenberg.

A further question. Do you recall playing or recording Mendelssohn Opus 13?

Oh, yes! It's one of our favorite pieces.

You know, I thought I had played every quartet ever written, but I heard a recording of that and thought it was Opus 130 of Beethoven. It turned out to be Opus 13 of Mendelssohn! So I *have* to attribute that to your playing. There's a quality that . . . you mean to say it just happens? I don't believe it! The Guarneri does something more than any quartet I've ever heard. I can analyze it technically: man-for-man superiority (there are no weak players); the inner parts are allowed to express themselves; the concept of the leading violinist with the others filling in is completely gone.

If we had one credo to express, and only one, it would have to be that. It would never have occurred to us that one player was ever more important than another, except for those moments that are dictated by the music itself. People have written about art in authoritarian states. They might just as well write about music in a string quartet where one man's personality predominates over the others.

That's the first thing that knocked me out with the Guarneri. To go on . . . have you matured as a quartet in ways that you could explain?

I have been very disappointed on occasion, in hearing a recording of ours, because we wouldn't play that way now. And even that Beethoven cycle we feel is terribly dated.

From last year?

No, no, I mean the records that we've made. Unfortunately, they live for a long time. They came relatively early in our careers, and perhaps some of them came a little too soon.

Anyhow, records are never more than kind of a shadow.

In what ways have you matured as a quartet?

Just the process of playing together all these years brings about a certain assuredness. We know each other well. We're able to read each other quite well, now. We have an almost sixth sense about each other, and I sometimes feel I can tell how somebody's going to start a work by the way he walks out onto the stage.

I wish you would cover that part a little more thoroughly. We brought it up once before. When two or more instruments make an entrance . . . I think it was you who brought out that you actually feel things together. If I remember correctly, ESP was mentioned.

Again, that brings me right back to this question of being leaderless. It's much easier to follow a lead, but then it always comes a shade late, and it's often somewhat tentative. But what we try to do is to lead together, and that is a physical thing. It's a question of breathing. It's almost a psychic thing, as well—hard to clarify and certainly hard to teach. I wouldn't know how to attack that problem in working with young players, for example, unless we first understood the principle involved. And the principle is that the quartet should breathe as one player and not follow, as in the role of, say, an accompanist at the piano playing with a singer.

Now, that's a fresh viewpoint that I think a lot of people will be interested in. You've now come to the nub of the whole question.

Any great accompanist would tell you that he (or she) breathes with the singer. Gerald Moore, let's say, or somebody who has lived and worked with great singers and played the great cycles. An accompanist who, on the other hand, isn't particularly interested in making music as chamber music but just in accompanying, will manage to stay as closely as he or she can with the solo voice, but it's always in a subordinate role.

Do you recall ever reading about Fritz Kreisler saying

that a lot of his success as a player was owed to his accompanist? He must have breathed with Kreisler. He didn't accompany. It's like when Menuhin used to give recitals with Baller. I think some people went as much to hear Baller play with that beautiful lyric tonal sense and security.

But, you see, that presupposes a certain amount of risk, too. You take chances doing that. Now, the other day, Arnold (Steinhardt) did something unexpected in the Opus 131. We played out in Oakland. And in the middle of the rather fast movement there comes a *fermata* bar, rather suddenly, and then I always expect that the attack after the *fermata* will come in very quickly—almost like a singer taking a quick breath and coming right in. But Arnold didn't do that, and I almost fell off my chair, because I had committed myself. And so, of course, I immediately had to backtrack. John* caught what was going on across the quartet and almost died laughing. I could see his face redden. But that's an example of the chances that we take because we don't merely follow one person's ideas of what the music should be.

I don't know if this advice is too good for Saturday-night players!

It depends on . . .

. . . the Saturday night and the players!

They should have at least an inkling of what goes on. Of course, first they have to learn the ABC's of quartet playing and that means that everybody has to know their parts. I know. I'm being a little bit . . .

. . . too hopeful.

Well, no. Look, I'm a hack tennis player.

That's a very good analogy.

And that has taught me an awful lot about music, believe me. You know the word "rachmunis"?

---

*John Dalley, Second Violinist

44

Yes, an understanding for somebody else's weaknesses. "Have rachmunis on that poor guy."

That's right. Rachmunis comes . . .

He aims at the ball and nearly hits it . . . beautiful swing, but never hits the ball.

Well, I consider myself a Saturday-night-type-tennis-player in that I could never aspire to be a really fine tennis player, but I love the game and I'm as enthusiastic as most of my friends are who play chamber music at home, and who carry the little book so that they know in any city in America they can call a perfect stranger and find themselves playing quartets that night. You know, the "directory."

One more question. To what extent do you feel your identity as a player is bound up in the Guarneri Quartet, or do you resent that?

Resent it? No, I'm grateful every moment.

I mean, if somebody said, "Oh, Michael Tree, the violist in the Guarneri Quartet," and not, "Oh, Michael Tree, the violist?"

I'd be very proud. I feel I'm a quarter of the Guarneri Quartet. And I feel that I'm partially responsible for the quartet's excellence. It's our baby, part of our artistic life.

I can't think of a better way to make music.

THE SECOND VIOLIN

To the possible surprise of many an amateur player, whose attitude often seems to be, "Well, since I'm letting 'Harry' play first violin in this quartet, I can relax. I've got the easy part," the second violin is a vital position with a *pivotal* function.

In contrast to the above attitude (which immediately dooms a quartet to mediocrity), the enlightened amateur, and certainly the professional, second violin has learned that the vitality of his performance can make or break the quartet.

Much is demanded of the second violin. Ideally, the technical facility required of the first violin should be

John Dalley, second violinist of the Guarneri Quartet.

brought to this second violin position. However, confidence in one's ability (from practicing and "psyching" oneself into a comfortable relationship with the instrument, which should be an extension of the self) will carry the player toward the goal. An understanding of the music and a keen awareness of what each of the others is doing are essential elements and are gained through the use of scores, as well as through increasing experience.

The second violin who plays with authority provides the quartet with rhythmic leadership, a prime requisite to maintaining ensemble. This then frees the first violin to concentrate on the technical demands of the part and on the interpretation to give the music. Providing the rhythmic and harmonic background to the leading part is usually done in conjunction with one or more of the other three instruments, so, as second violin, you try to match style and tone quality with the others. Your alertness and awareness must be maintained. In order to match, you must watch each other for entrances and listen to each other for style and tone. Be ready when you are needed to reinforce the harmony or the rhythm or to create a musical "bas relief" by fading into an *obbligato*.

Often the second violin is charged with rhythmic support of the first violin. This is usually accomplished in conjunction with the viola. There is the classical, typically Mozartean type of background rhythm – eighth-note repetition. It is important that it not sound like a Kreutzer exercise (or any other kind, for that matter), but that there be expressive rhythm which follows the flow of the quartet itself. For example, in some types of melodies, one would accent the first of four (YUM, pum, pum, pum). Next comes the generation of the type of rhythm that fits in with the spirit of the quartet – in its harmony and in its melody – such as the Schubert, Opus 29, "The Swan," where the first violin is playing a very flowing melody accompanied by a beautiful lyric counterpoint in the second violin. The cello and viola may either play a very sharp "sec" *spiccato* rhythm for contrast or, to increase the overall *lusingando* and beautiful Schubertean lyricism, play just the opposite — sort of a *flottato spiccato* (ya.ta.ta.ta). This is a general illustration of how many kinds of bowing an accompanying part can create. It is important that you be aware of the variety of possibilities, and that you actively contribute to the decisions made.

Stasis is anathema to a quartet! There is simply no such thing as seeing a stretch of eighth-notes or a long note and saying to oneself, "Well, I'll just let it go through and keep it in tune and play along with it." What gives a quartet its character and differentiation is that the so-called inner parts have roles to play just as important as the outer solo part and the extreme bass. In this connection, you never just *hold* a note. You have to vibrate it almost constantly, and these long, held, extended tones have to fluctuate and weave in and out with the harmony to make the entire sense of the quartet move. If the quartet seems to stand still, something is missing — is not being done. There is *no* such thing as a "static quartet." To keep things moving, more can be done by the inner parts than by the solo outside parts. The participation of the inner parts must be dynamic. There is no greater sin for the inner parts than for them to just sit there and either rumble away with their yum.pum.pum.pum or hold a note for three or four measures without doing anything with it!

When the lead plays its melody and then comes to a note that is held, the second violin and viola either bring in notes that are missing or emphasize the harmony or make a little swell and *decrescendo*. At every opportunity, little notes that form part of the melody or counter melody or a sort of a canon or an imitation of a solo part must be brought out. Even the so-called boring, long, held notes have a thousand infinite variations of *crescendi, decrescendi,* changes of tone color, changes of length of bow, and all of the other various arts with which the stringed instrument can be played that will make the part interesting.

Conversely, many quartets are written with the thoughts of the composer divided up among the four parts, especially in the later Beethoven quartets and in more modern music. The classic idea of one supreme melody accompanied by lesser parts is no longer the prime objective of the quartet. The much more subtle rendering. of the composer's thoughts, where the quartet is subdivided and is projected through all four parts, is found in the late Beethoven quartets, the Ravel, and, indeed, in the majority of modern quartets where we now have a definite interplay between all four parts.

Special attention now must be paid to the fact that the first violin may play just four or five notes of a melody and then smoothly fade away, while the second violin or viola or cello brings out the next four notes of the melody and this may go on so that the first brings out the next four, etc. Now we have four risings and fallings of the melody itself. We can divide again because the *obbligato* melody also is changing. Whereas in the first example, the first violin is playing the very important actual melody that the composer intended, the second violin is playing an *obbligato* which is equally important.

When the second violin changes over to playing the premier melody, the first may become the *obbligato*. Quality of tone has to change so that the total effect is of one violin playing, accompanied by the same quality of *obbligato*. Further, this effect holds good for viola and cello combined with all the other possible instrument groupings.

When you get into some of the late Beethoven quartets or into modern composers, the playing of string quartets becomes so complex and so subtle that it is like a very, very complicated chess game. Furthermore, this business of solo and *obbligato* is but a small part of what's going on. While the second violin and first violin may be counterplaying, along with the viola, back and forth between solo and *ob-bligato*, the cello may be playing an entirely different counter melody. Again, we don't want the cello player to just sit there and say, "Well, it's marked *piano*, so I really mustn't be heard." Whenever an instrument has a melody, a counter melody, an important *obbligato* or a counter harmony, it should be played with a quality of tone that borders on solo.

This brings us to one of the most important aspects of the supreme thrills and objectives of quartet playing—the qualities of tone to be brought out and how each instrument should balance the way it produces its tone with what's going on in the other three. Above all, in a string quartet one never plays orchestrally. There are never to be any orchestral attacks; no *crunching*. At all times, one endeavors to produce the most beautiful tone one is capable of, in a blend with the other instruments, so that the sound itself is warm and glowing.

Take the Ravel string quartet as a prime example. This starts out clearly enough with the upper solo part in the first violin accompanied by typical Ravelian harmonies, and so the first phrase is covered. Then comes the expansion into more modern harmonies. During this phase, all four parts are of equal importance. A figuration starts between the second violin and viola of running sixteenths in very unusual intervals. This figuration creates the effect of harmonic undulations, unusual tonal effects and, at the same time, the whole atmosphere is rather subdued.

An emanation of sound never before encountered in string quartet playing is achieved. On top of the running figures shared by second violin and viola, we have these unusual harmonies and the rising and falling in dynamics. Here, it's up to the second violin and viola to achieve a particular type of sound, usually known as the French type, where one plays closer to the bridge, with more edge to the sound, and emphasizes the intervals. To contrast and make the difference clearer—if it were, for example, Brahms— one could take almost the same figures and have them run along at full bravura tone, as in the Brahms concerto and many other Brahms works. But this is modern French, and we want a different quality of tone.

You can experiment with various ways of achieving the tone, as long as you keep the objective in mind. It is certainly a challenge to the finest players to get such a blend between second violin and viola that they achieve a weird effect, through the use of unusual tonalities suffused with undulating *crescendi* and *decrescendi*, so that the listener is carried off to new realms of harmony.

Now we balance this off against the first violin who's wandering high up on the E string with a fresh type of melody new to quartet music. Here, the challenge to second violin and viola is to follow the line of playing by the first violin. With their rise and fall of running notes, they contrast, contribute, or blend with what the first is doing, so that the whole achieves an effect that is greater than any one of the parts.

This is a sample of the kinds of things that are a supreme challenge. It is far from the typical concept of the role of the second violin in the quartet.

Interview with John Dalley, Second Violinist

First of all, how do you regard the role of the second violin in quartet playing, in general?

The role of the second violinist in a quartet should be one of liberating the first violinist so the first can dispense with so many of the duties that the old-time first violinists had. But, you know, that works two ways. He has to play with a first violinist who will willingly relinquish some of these duties. In the older quartets, the first violinist conducted everything from bar to bar. He was, in effect, a concertmaster, a leader, a conductor. When he's doing this constantly, it takes away from some of the spontaneity, I think,

51

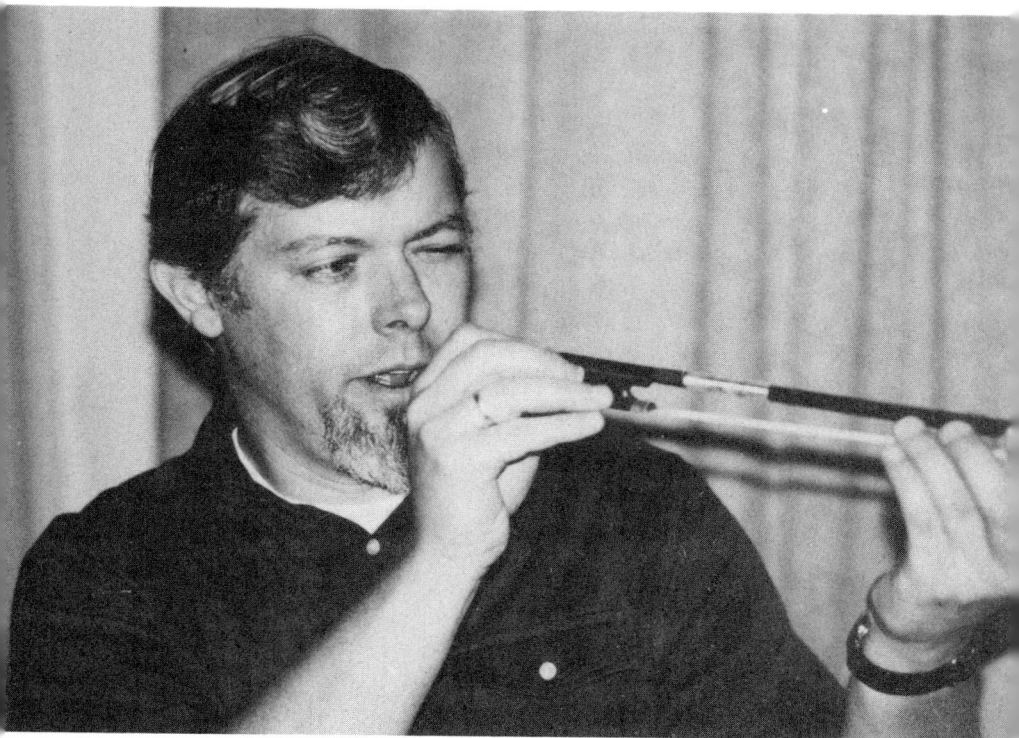

John Dalley, second violinist.

of his own part. So the second violin can, in a sense, be like a mini-conductor who can control the lower three voices, or it can be done in pairs according to how the music is written at that time.

He can, certainly in Haydn quartets, liberate the first violinist from having constantly to occupy himself with what the other voices are playing. Because the first violinist should be free (especially in Haydn) to play as he wants to, the second violinist has to be kind of a mind-reader and transmit that to the others. We have found that often it does not work for the cello to do a great deal of leading, because it's difficult for the cello to lead. I think there are some basic problems because he's rooted to the floor. So the obvious choice is the second violin. And since he has quite a bit less to do than the first violin in terms of notes on the page, he can become a conductor. But, it's a subtle thing. It's not visible, where you see the second violinist conducting constantly. It should be subtle. And he would be doing this throughout the classical works . . . through Beethoven, Haydn, Mozart.

My next question: how do you feel about playing in the Guarneri Quartet where you can really rely on the skill, knowledge and experience of the other participants — where there are no weak members?

It's a true democracy, because no one person has the ultimate say over the others. And when it comes to performance, it's entirely a matter of who's got the ball. When Dave (David Soyer, Cellist) has solo voices, we will follow him. I don't mean play behind him, but follow him — he will be leading. Sometimes I will be giving rhythmic leads at the same time, which is still part of my function, so this frees the cello from having to do that. Of course, the role of the inner voices is something else. We can get into that later.

Yes, we'll get into it.

Moreover the second violinist really . . . or at least in our quartet . . . should control the inner voices – in a rhythmic sense but not necessarily in an interpretive sense.

We'd be interested to know your opinion of how your group maintains its perfection of ensemble.

What perfection is that?

You're certainly noted for being a totally balanced ensemble. In fact, it's almost a unique group tone. How do you achieve this, and how do you maintain it?

Well, a lot has to do with, I think, one's upbringing and the musicological influences in one's early life. I think the four of us had fairly similar influences, musically.

Very interesting! Each of you has a fresh approach to these same questions.

For example, if we were to sit down, with a new fourth player, one who was trained, say, in Germany, we would have a problem, because he would, ninety-nine per cent of the time, have a different concept of sound, bowing strokes, and, to a certain extent, freedom. Sometimes you go too far, and it becomes bad taste. I think sometimes we may tend to exaggerate more than somebody who's European-trained and in particular, German-trained. German musicians tend to be very much more on an even plane as far as interpretive details are concerned. They don't exaggerate a great deal, whereas we do, especially in romantic music.

And you would say such a similar background and concept of what you're playing serves to balance the total tone and the interpretation and . . . you do achieve, somehow, a tremendous group tone – I don't mean by volume, but rather a balanced resonance.

Yet the four of us don't sound the least bit alike. You still have four players. But there's still something about the heritage . . . the influences of certain people – teachers and so forth – plus styles of bowing . . . and tone production that tends to bind us together. We also dig in a lot. We play in large halls and for large audiences, so we don't minimize anything. We're always maximizing.

54

As a group, do you all like everything you play . . . for instance, the Lutoslawski thing that you did the other night? Or do you sometimes play things that somebody doesn't particularly admire? Do you select what you're going to play on the basis of what everyone likes?

The answer to that is, "Yes and no." Most of the time we do like what we're playing. There may be one of us who is less enthusiastic about a certain work. The Lutoslawski is a good case in point, because I know that two out of the four are not really as wild about the piece as the other two (I won't say who those are). But, you see, it's a give and take, and you have to decide, "All right, this piece is good enough to travel with." I mean, anybody can sit down and play a piece once, but when you travel a whole year with something, you've really got to like it. So if one of us doesn't really like a work that much, he may have to live with it at least for a season.

You know the impression I received as I sat in the audience when you played the Lutoslawski?

What?

That one of the big reasons you were playing it was that it was really a fresh challenge to keep up your interest, because it was so different that you couldn't go to sleep for a tenth of a second. You had to be aware at all times, and it was sort of a jar to keep your musical interests alive.

Are you speaking as a listener?

Yes, I mean looking at you and having a good idea of what's going on up there.

It's not nearly as much fun to play as it is to hear. I first heard the Lutoslawski, and the effect was much more startling as a listener than I had later as a player. As a player, you lose some of the interplay in the voices from bar to bar. Of course, you know, Lutoslawski doesn't want his work played the same way twice. He has written it out deliberately so that you cannot do so. There is no score, in the traditional sense, and each player is encouraged to play freely within each section.

Well, that's why I say, doesn't that tend to keep up your interest in the piece, as such?

It does.

That was the impression I got. I felt that one of the reasons you were playing this is that it isn't "the same old Haydn every time." It's something fresh. Because you're going to have to play maybe a hundred times a season, once in a while you stick in this Lutoslawski. It puts you on your toes again for a while.

I personally find the Lutoslawski much more fascinating than the Schubert (E-flat Maj.) that we played. I don't find the Schubert a varied work. I find it tonally monotonous because it hovers around E flat for twenty-five minutes. It has lovely things, but it's a very sleepy work, and you have to really be in the mood and really love it, whereas the Lutoslawski has things that jar you and hold your interest.

Exactly as I suspected.

I'm not saying the Lutoslawski is a greater work, but for me, at this moment, I find it a more fascinating piece than the Schubert.

It's more of a challenge.

Yes.

Now, concerning the control of the dynamic range – just as an example – how? why? when? I'm thinking about the Saturday-night-players who get together once a week and play Beethoven's Op. 59, No. 3, once every two years, after which they feel they've been through the quartet range. So, when you're explaining questions like this, think of *them*, because this evaluation is not for players of your caliber. How do you control your dynamic range or any other range of expression? Or *is* there a control? Please attack it from all angles.

First of all there is a control. It's a kind of distilling process where four voices or four instruments become one. It becomes a given dynamic at a given time. More specifically the character of the melody or phrase often determines the dynamics, and the lead voice or solo voice has the final say. Of course, the old saying "If you can't hear the solo voice, you are too loud" always applies.

I asked Soyer if you would perform differently in a small room . . . if you would then come down to a real triple *pianissimo*. And he said, "No, we play the same way in a big hall or a small room—same dynamics."

Yes, that's true. Since we do have the capacity to play extremely loud, we don't perhaps utilize the softer range of dynamics as much as we could. The old concept of the quartet player who sits back and plays a kind of nice, "gemütlich" *mezzo forte* all the way through is something that you have to get away from. You have to take the equipment you've got and utilize it to the maximum. You also have to be able to control it to the maximum.

Now you've reached a point that's very interesting. Could you expand a little more? Basically I am talking about intellectual control and physical control; intellectual decisions made prior to performances, and physical or technical control during performances. And so on a somewhat higher plane, I am thinking about these control factors being applied uniformly by the four quartet members.

Following the trend of what you've just been saying, I just thought of this question: In a way are you also saying that now, since the liberation of the inner voices, you can achieve much more sound because the inner voices are allowed to let go?

That's right. Absolutely.

Now there's another viewpoint. The difference between your *piano* and your *forte* seems to be more a matter of tone color than it does dynamics. The *piano* has a *piano* sound to it, but it's still just as audible.

Yes. That may be because we tend to play a maximum *piano* too much. Then again, it may be because we play in large halls.

Just as an aside, what I'm trying to expound in this book is that quartets have evolved a long way from the 19th century Joachim Quartet—the virtuoso soloist accompanied by three lesser players—until it has come to the point where composers are writing for four artists . . . individual concertos for four artists. And the players are four concert artists making a four-part concerto out of the music.

Yes.

The amazing part is that you've carried this idea to great heights. We understand it when you're getting to Ravel and you're going forward—Bartók and so on—but now you've applied it backwards and you play Mozart the same way. It's wonderful!

Yes. I remember an incident that happened in Germany. We were recording for a radio station an early Mozart quartet. The light went on, we got the signal and began to play. About twenty seconds into the first movement, the engineer, who was sitting back in the control room, spoke to us over the intercom. He said, "Achtung, bitte, das ist nicht Mozart!" So he interrupted us and in effect was lecturing us on the fact that we had no idea how to play Mozart. I don't remember the specifics, but he said everything was too much—too much this, too much that. And it became very apparent when we heard the first playback that the microphones were placed very close to us. When you play at maximum, with the adrenalin going, you're playing for the back rows—why, it overpowers a microphone. Plus the fact that he didn't like the way we played Mozart, either.

This is another aside, but this very thing you're talking about is what gave me the inspiration that this book needed to be written. More than 30 years ago when I came to New York as a student, I was always organizing quartets. We'd play Mozart, and they'd look at me. I'd keep exhorting the second violin and viola, "Come on! Come on! Play! Play!" They ignored me. We'd get finished and they'd say, "Now, really that's not the way you play Mozart." So what could I do? I waited and waited, and then along came the Guarneri, and I said, "*That's* the way! The message has got to be written down. Somebody's got to put it down!"

If we fail in any facet of our performance, I think we fail in the ability to allow the solo voice to have a dynamic freedom. You see, we're very reluctant to let the other guy have a clear shot. Don't forget, in a quartet of equals, you have four egos going in high gear all the time.

That's very noticeable. You need a super violinist up there. Arnold*, of course, is first rate.

You know, in the old days, a violinist would perhaps gather three other players and form a quartet. Joachim was a case in point . . . I think he traveled from town to town, would pick up three local players wherever he was, and that would be the Joachim Quartet for the evening. But, nowadays, as you know, four people get together and, hopefully, are evenly matched.

Of course, that's the big issue.

The Griller Quartet was a good example of a quartet of equals – an excellent quartet. They should have had a much greater following than they had. They deserved more.

All right, now the answer to this question should again be directed to our Saturday-nighters. How closely do you follow each other in bowings and phrasings, and so on? You know, there's that old concept that everybody should play down bow or up bow in a certain phrase or the same style of bowing.

We don't do that as much as other groups. Once again, it's that feeling of the individual. We want to keep our individuality, and if we feel we can imitate something using another stroke or another direction, why, we go ahead and do it. So, frequently we do have bowings that seem opposite.

*Arnold Steinhardt, First Violinist

So, your advice to the Saturday-nighters is?

It depends. It's a very difficult question because even four amateurs who get together are not going to play *spiccato* the same way. You might have one person who feels more comfortable playing up bows—up, up, up, up—and the other prefers down, up, down, up. The trick is to duplicate each other's sound, and if it can be done successfully that way, then it's all right, in my opinion. Just as there is no one way to hold the bow. You can hold it a myriad of ways, as long as you can do with the bow what you have to do. So there are no hard and fast rules.

The last question I have is this: are you always in top form, or do the circumstances or the places where you play inspire or depress you?

Well, the four of us, I'm sure, are never in top form at the same instant. We also don't react to a given concert the same way. And, of course, on tour we don't tire the same way. I mean, if we're on tour for two-and-a-half weeks, somebody could be extremely tired on a particular night, but the other person may not be. That's part of the game. I think it's safe to say the music itself does or should inspire you.

Do you ever have nights when everything seems to gel just right, and the more it goes, the better you play, and it builds up to an inspirational climax? Has that ever been the case?

Sometimes. I've sensed that things have been almost optimum for a given work, but not necessarily for a complete concert. I felt the other night that we played one work . . . I can't remember which one it was . . . quite well.

Was that the concert with the Haydn Op. 77, No. 1 or No. 2, or Alban Berg?

We play so many, I can't remember, but I do recall thinking, *This seems to be going better than it usually does.* The rest of the concert wasn't on that level, however. You see, if you asked the four of us immediately after a concert, specifically if this was better or that was better, you'd get four answers. Seldom do we agree on these things.

60

Then, that *is* your answer? That you don't feel, as a group, that some great inspiration came out that evening for some reason?

No, inspirational moments do emerge but not all the way through the concert. I remember the first time we played the Beethoven cycle, which must have been 12 or so years ago. We played one of the concerts of the cycle. We were playing those three Beethovens for the first time, and I thought it went very well. I was very happy about it. I remember coming offstage after Opus 74, the "Harp" Quartet, saying, "That was terrific!" and the other three looked at me in absolute horror, crying, "You don't know what you're saying! That was just awful!" What I liked about it was that it had a lot of spontaneity and freshness, because, in a sense, it was somewhat under-rehearsed. Well, I can't remember when we've played it better. We may have played it more accurately in certain ways, but I don't think it had the life that it had that first time.

Now you're on your own, and you can start elaborating on this spontaneity or on any general ideas about quartet playing.

Spontaneity is a whole new subject. You achieve spontaneity in different ways at different times because you're four players, not one.

That gives me an idea for a question. Is your playing, then, the exact opposite of what one might call a "rigid setting?" Isn't that what you've been saying? Spontaneity means that everybody has boundaries, but they're not rigid.

What I was thinking about was the spontaneity in which four people seem to be inspired in the same way at a given time. That's very hard to achieve, and I don't think it's possible to achieve that more than just momentarily. In other words, that would be the ultimate if it occurred for an hour-and-a-half at night. I don't think it could ever be that way. But, that's part of the romance about it . . . you're always striving for it.

Arnold Steinhardt, first violinist of the Guarneri Quartet.

THE FIRST VIOLIN

The function of the first violin is a subject of considerable controversy. A great weight of tradition and assumption backs the historical role of the first violin. It would seem that only the master composers and a relative minority of players have realized the enlightened role of the first violin. Although this book espouses the latter view, along with the Guarneri Quartet who actualize it, we will dwell on the historical outlook in some depth inasmuch as it is an entrenched view—one that lingers still in European chamber music and that dominates the experience of the average casual quartet player.

Traditionally, it has been up to the first violin to *initiate* the general course of action of the quartet, to delineate the style, to suggest the mood and set the rhythm. The following analogy perhaps best sums up the historical view of the first violin in a quartet:

We can compare the playing of a string quartet to the maneuvering of a ship through the ocean. Let us take a racing yacht making the ocean voyage from America to England—say the Lipton Cup Race—where we have a captain in charge and a crew of three. The crew is very important. Each one has his own job to do and he must do it perfectly in order to reach the destination first. One may be in charge of the sails, another in charge of adjusting the rudder and the stays in order to get the best advantage of the wind, and a third may be watching the angle of the ship itself so that it will take most advantage of the oncoming waves. *But* it is the captain—the first violin—who has the overall picture, who has to look ahead and, with, presumably, his knowledge and experience, know what this cloudbank means, what that current means, see the squall coming up and steer the ship and give his commands to the crew to take the best advantage of sailing, whether it is through the calm seas of a Dittersdorf quartet, or the stormy waves of a late Beethoven.

Now we begin to see more clearly the actual function of the first violin as he steers our beautiful yacht, the string quartet, through the seas. Just as the best sailor is the one who knows how best to take advantage of the currents, winds, wind directions, wave directions, squalls, smooth seas and rough seas, so it is the first violin in a string quartet who, by taking the best advantage of the juxtaposition of all the tone colors, the harmonies, the *crescendi*, the *staccati*, the types of bowing, the emphasizing of various lines of melody and harmony, will be the best navigator, that is the best interpreter, of that particular piece of music. It is the first violinist's duty to carry out this role of transmission of his knowledge, his personality to the crew — to the rest of the members of the quartet.

This analogy derives from the tradition of early (and some later) string quartets and is applicable to the casual string quartet group where leadership remains essential in order to achieve the best possible cohesion and musical sense.

However, a quantum leap must be taken to progress from this prevailing attitude to the evolving awareness, by players and composers alike, of the extraordinary potential of the string quartet form. It is not simply a matter of stretching the "captain" analogy to fit each player as he or she takes the lead. In fact, the analogy becomes obsolete. No longer do we have merely a vehicle for solo violin and three accomplished, but undistinguished, players rendering a suitable accompaniment. Nor is the first violin saddled with the dual responsibility of meeting the technical demands of its part while at the same time conducting the work. Rather, we now have four emancipated soloists who, with keen insight, constant awareness, expert capabilities, merge their individual functions into a single instrument. They become an unmatched musical phenomenon, realizing artistic achievements beyond the scope of any other medium.

The first violin is now free to solo because others take the lead to maintain the ensemble. It can take off — soar — and the group will propel and support that. The first can, in turn, take the lead and, in so doing, determine the style, the mood, the tempo.

For instance, in setting style, Mozart can be played in many moods, from full sonority to delicate *spiccato*, from a slow tempo to a sizzling liveliness. In fact, after listening to about two dozen quartets, one realizes that Mozart—or any composer—can be played in an infinity of styles.

The same holds for setting the tonal level. The Grieg quartet, for example, can be played in a heavy-handed, triple *forte* manner, or it can be played in a much more delicate manner, avoiding the triple *forti*. Then, when it finally does build up to a climax, the result is much more effective and alters the musical structure into what one might call a better composition.

In taking the lead, then, the first violin can introduce a new mood, an altered tempo, a little more *rubato*, a slightly different style and revitalize the quartet presentation. Whether leading or soaring, it can impel the quartet into regions where the musical totality exceeds in beauty the mundane notes which are there on paper.

Interview with Arnold Steinhardt, First Violinist

What do you consider the role of the first violin in a string quartet to be?

Historically, the first violin was the leader of the group. He was the one who set the *tempi*, gave the leads. Often he was the dominant musical personality. But in our age, as we've begun to play more and more chamber music and love it more and perhaps understand it more, I think we're gravitating less and less to that idea. In our group where we are really a republic of equals I'm certainly not the leader. There are no leaders. That is not even a question in our group. You hear it often as a lingering tradition in Europe. In England I'm often called the leader, and in Germany I'm called the *primarius*, just traditionally. Actually it makes

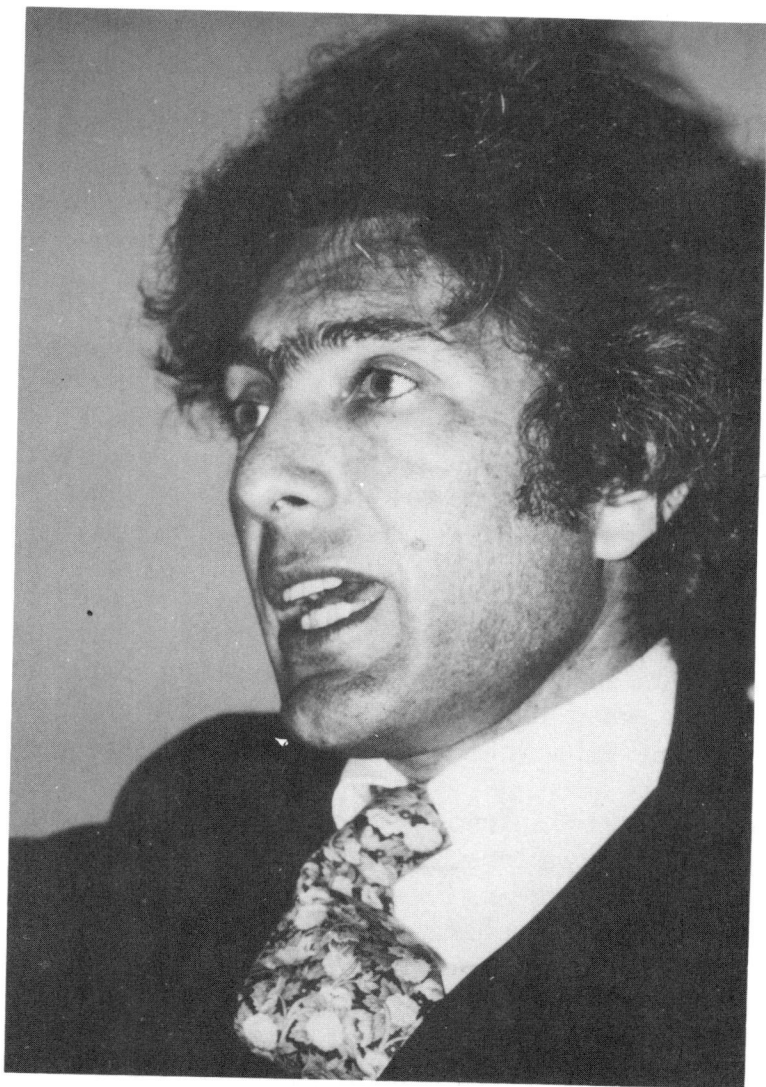

Arnold Steinhardt, first violinist. .

me wince a little bit, because it's certainly not so.

Please keep in mind that this is not an interview of one musicologist for another musicologist. It's for what we call the Saturday-night-bunch. You know, they get together once a week, and if they play Op. 59, No. 3 once every two years, they think they've gone through the repertoire.

We can afford not to have any leaders in our group because there are no weak links in the chain. There are four dominant, independent personalities . . . strong, independent personalities. However, the realities of chamber music are that you sit down to read and not everybody is so lucky to have four equal links in the chain. If there is a stronger link in the chain, it's good that that personality takes a leading role. I don't think that's necessarily bad. It's practical.

That was my next question. Does the tremendous inner strength of the Guarneri help you in your rendition, in your interpretation of the various works? Does it release you more instead of tying you in to conducting?

Me, personally? Oh, absolutely. In this group, anybody who has the lead voice, whether it be me or any of the others, is free to take flight. Because one does have that assurance that the other people not only have their parts down cold and are technically very self-assured, but that they have enough experience and sensitivity to adjust. As a matter of fact, one interesting technical point about our group is that often, when one voice will have the solo, other voices will lead, will take care of this mundane business of everybody being together. For example, when I have the solo, often John will give leads, and I'll follow him at the start so that I can just be free to play and not worry about ensemble.

This is a very refreshing viewpoint. John mentioned that as a second violin, many times he takes the role of conductor.

That's absolutely right.

This frees you (or your violin) if you want to do little things here and there. He takes over the mundane chores.

He often does it because the first violin has a tendency to

play the tune more. But if John is playing, and we are accompanying, I'll find myself in John's position and then I'll be the leader because I'm suddenly the second violin or one of the accompanying voices.

When you are creating more and more of a sound . . . there's something about your ensemble. You've built it up. There's so much strength on all four sides that finally we get an ensemble sound such as I've never before heard in quartet playing. Do you attribute this to the individual strength of each individual player, or is it the working out—the fact that nobody's left to play "mmp, buh, buh, buh," but everybody's *playing*?

The latter, I think. Everybody plays. There's none of the feeling of subsidiary roles. Even accompanying voices are treated with great attention and given their due; harmonic figures, rhythmic figures . . .

And, of course, as you get into more modern music, it definitely is a concerto for four artists. The other thing that amazes me is that you have also applied this principle inversely. You play Mozart the same way—like a concerto—and the result is just beautiful. Now, is that an outgrowth of your gradual recognition of the way to play quartets, or is it something that you chose—that there are no subsidiary parts—everybody is just as important?

It's not that everybody's just as important. There are times when one voice *should* come out and everything else remain somewhat in the background. But it's really difficult to make any hard and fast rules about it. There are no generalizations.

How about quality of tone? Who generates the quality of tone, especially in a tone—poem piece such as the Ravel, where you're changing tone qualities all the time?

You know, there's no one person . . . it is a result. Everybody plays, and then you hear the sound that comes out and immediately you adjust and there is some place somewhere in the middle of the quartet—an imaginary place, in the air—you reach for to find that sound. But we don't sit down and say, "Now, I want a rich, juicy, thick sound, here," or "I'd like a gossamer sound," or "What's our philosophy of sound here?" We don't have a philosophy of sound. Our philosophy, if anything, is to seek every individual place and treat it for what it is.

So you let the music itself carry you in tone quality. Is that the way?

I would say so. I try not to have any preconceived ideas about doing anything. It sometimes, of course, becomes an intellectual exercise we can get into, in a way. But, it is as if when we are playing something, we realize, "Aha! These are the possibilities!" Mind you, we'll argue about which the proper sound is—whether it should be rich and juicy or quieter or played more delicately or whatever—but it's usually done as a pragmatic thing. After you've heard it, then you talk about it.

I would like to end this by saying that I have heard the so-called best quartets in the world, and they're *not* balanced. I won't mention names, but in a recent quartet, the viola player stuck out like a sore thumb, and the second violinist played like a second violinist. The Guarneri however has a certain agglutination of sounds where you gradually build up until you achieve results that I have never before heard.

The artistic seriousness the members of the Guarneri Quartet bring to the music they perform is evident from this photograph of one of their concerts.

THE APPLICATION OF TECHNIQUES

Master musicians utilize a myriad of techniques to achieve the finest performances. This book has referred to and delineated many of these in the descriptions of the functions of each of the quartet instruments. In this section, The Application of Techniques, specific instruction is offered on the techniques to apply in the production of particular works. Once assimilated in the context in which it is here presented, this information can be applied to any quartet one may endeavor to play.

One of the most important concepts in string quartet playing is that of tone colors. A prime consideration at every moment of playing is the tone production of the individual instruments and of the instruments as a whole. We will define six different tone levels in string quartet playing.

The "primary" level would be the pure solo where it is definitely one of the four instruments proclaiming the theme in its purest form. We still must keep in mind that this is not the masterful spectacular fireworks of a violin soloist playing the Brahms Concerto with a massive symphony orchestra. Although the string quartet soloist is definitely the star (the shining example in his proclamation of the theme that he is expounding), he still is part of an intimate ensemble, and the other three instruments must always be kept in mind. Such a tone within so small an ensemble might be likened to light-refraction from a finely faceted gem: brilliant but contained.

The subtleties start, however, when we try to answer the question, "What kinds of tones do the remaining instruments produce?" Suppose we are playing Borodin's Second String Quartet with the first violin way up on the E string in the lovely slow movement. Obviously he's playing with a pure solo tone. Now, in this very melody there are a lot of counter melodies going on in the second violin, viola, and cello. What kinds of tone quality are called into play as these instruments vary back and forth from accompanying *obbligato*, to counter playing, to *contraobbligato*, and so forth?

We have first what we will call a "counter solo" where, for instance, the first violin pauses on a long note, and the second violin or viola interjects an answer. The answer should be done with full solo quality. Emphasis is placed on the word "quality" because that does *not* mean volume. What is needed is solo quality equal to that of the first violin. The player uses full *vibrato* and big bows.

This brings us to another facet of tone production in the instruments that don't have the obvious solo, which would be a very prominent counter melody, or *solo obbligato*. For instance, a viola might play a counter solo against another instrument, or the second violin might be playing along with a solo part of any of the other three instruments. Unless he matches the tone production and phrasing of the solo, half the beauty of that particular phrase is lost. It is just at this point where the second violin may tend to let himself be outshown that the absolute reverse should be accentuated. That is, while still being an *obbligato*—still being number two in the production of that particular phrase—the second violin should, within reason, be producing beautiful phrases, beautiful tones, *crescendi* and *decrescendi*, and be anything but static. At every possible chance he should bring out a little solo phrase. The tone weaving is to be blended. The same type of *vibrato*, the same type of surging solo quality should be manifested in a manner equaling the top soloist. There's more ensemble in such a type of musical construction, so we do not have the most spectacular type of solo tone, but rather more of an ensemble tone, still with plenty of *vibrato* and individualistic tone.

Next, there might be an *obbligato* part by the violins or other blend of instruments playing a combination of tones and ensemble against the lead solo. This should also be played with plenty of *vibrato*, but not quite a *solo vibrato*, and with the performer keeping in mind that it is an *obbligato*. On the other hand, it should be stressed and not thrown away. At this level, also, sometimes the *obbligato* or the theme itself is broken up into fragments and thrown back and forth among the various instruments or combinations of instruments and when these few notes are played, they again should be brought out—not so much with volume of tone (although this can be used in a very fluent, subtle manner), but by means of individuality: a more soloistic type of *vibrato*, a little *crescendo* and any of the other countless means whereby phrases can be emphasized.

Then there is the level where we are definitely playing background music. Still, the background should not be played in the moribund manner such as one usually hears from the second violin in a hotel trio furnishing dinner music, where practically all he is doing is moving his bow back and forth, and if it comes out in the right place, well, that makes a good hotel orchestra. If not, who cares? If one wants to get really serious, plenty of the same thing goes on in the finest symphony orchestras. A goodly percentage of the string section is just playing the right notes in the right places. But even at this level, there will always be certain notes in the rhythm that should be emphasized. Many times, in music from Mozart to Webern, there is a rest— nobody is playing—and then a combination of two, such as second violin and viola or viola and cello, will start the rhythm going again. In this case, the rhythm must be set by the way they play . . . for instance, an accent of some type every four notes.

Now we come to one of the very foundations of quartet playing—the essence of quartet playing is that it is a unification of four *soloists*. It is not a background such as in orchestra playing or chamber music playing. Each individual is playing a solo part and, for this reason, no matter what each instrument is playing, the tone should *never* be dead. Nevertheless, it should always be blended with what the others are doing, while certain notes are to be especially brought out. To be precise, when chords are being played, almost invariably the sharp seventh should be emphasized with a little extra *vibrato* by the instrument playing in that chord. We will point to this exactly a little later on when we analyze in depth certain string quartets.

There is yet another level which, by itself, may seem almost unimportant. By this is meant a single sustained note which is held for some duration. Some of the most luminous moments in quartet playing are those in which the two violins and the viola are playing figurations and solos all over the fingerboard while the cello is simply holding a high A. For, if the cello holds this high A with a beautiful *vibrato* and sings along with the others—meeting their *crescendi* and *decrescendi* and bringing his part out with a glorious singing tone—we have again the difference between a mediocre and a superb performance.

We can now reduce this whole business of the varying types of tone production in quartet playing to a formula:

The Prime Solo, by any of the four instruments, proclaiming the theme and leading the quartet in every aspect—tone color, tempo, mood. Whatever the solo/leader does, the others instantly match. In a quartet there can be no time-lag between leader and "followers." The ideal performance is akin to the action of a flock of birds in flight. They change course simultaneously. There is no perceptible gap between the spark of initiation and the recognition and followthrough.

The Counter Solo, matching full solo quality in *answer*.

A Very Prominent Counter Melody, or *solo obbligato*, inter-weaving with the prime *solo*. Each employs essentially the same type of *vibrato*, the same type of surging quality, but the *obbligato solo* maintains a bit more of an ensemble, rather than solo, tone. He still effectively uses plenty of *vibrato* and injects a modicum of individuality.

A Counter Obbligato Part, for any of the instruments playing a combination of tones and ensemble against the solo part. It does not have the solo prominence, but it should be stressed and not submerged.

Definitely Background Music, but no diminution of vitality of sound. This is not a time for lackluster sound production or for hacking. There will always be certain notes in the rhythm that will be emphasized.

A Single Sustained Note, which, by itself, may seem almost unimportant.

RED-LINING

We have discussed the six types and levels of tone quality and phrasing that the individual member and the ensemble use in producing certain effects and in stressing certain parts which include whole melodies, *obbligati*, even leading tones and single notes in parts of phrases. We should here mention that in a great deal of music, either because of the laziness of the editor or composer, or the composer's feeling that the players are musicians enough to supply the dynamics that are not indicated, we find (in Mozart, for example) a *mezzo forte* in one part only and a *piano* four bars later and nothing in between. The dynamics are left to the interpreter.

Because stresses are a major factor in making music, it is most important that the players determine where these stresses should occur. This portion of the book is devoted to assisting the player in making such determinations and to suggesting how to implement them.

To indicate the amount and type of stress (which goes

from *vibrato* to *marcato* to a different type of bowing, more bow, less bow, *crescendo, decrescendo* and all the other multifarious ways of producing a totality of playing that ends up as quartet playing at its finest), we have resolved that the simplest, most effective method would be simply to use a red pen to underline that portion of your part which should be emphasized. For the sake of clarity, obvious solos or themes would not be red-lined; only the special or obscure phrases. The determinations of such stresses must be a joint venture with a group consensus on the effects you will strive to attain. Therefore, the score of the quartet is a virtual necessity. (Authors' note: the scores to all of the Mozart quartets are available in a single volume for a very reasonable price. The same is true of all the Beethoven quartets. We strongly urge such a purchase, even if only to refer to your part in the ensemble conceived by the composer. Use of scores in the manner suggested by this book will render them of inestimable worth to the serious quartet player.) Once you have agreed on where a highlight occurs (perhaps with the aid of this book or your favorite recording), you have the question of what type of stress and how much. The amount and type of effect achieved in the red-lined part would be determined by the player's experience, talent, technique, and by the very fact that, since the part is red-lined, he or she knows that it needs a special emphasis of some sort. In the final analysis, what the red line does is to remind the player that this particular phrase, note, etc., needs some kind of a special effect, whether it be *crescendo, vibrato,* or other emphasis.

We can, therefore, condense the entire analysis into a very few words. As a quartet, everyone together should go through the score and the individual parts and determine places that should be especially brought out. These places, whether complete phrases, parts of phrases, complete themes, even single notes, can be determined and, to a certain extent, the amount of stress ascertained before the quartet has even been sightread. Now when the quartet is played, the red line functions as a sort of directional arrow, serving the same purpose as the multitude of road signs we see when we drive up a curving mountain road: "curve to the left," "dip," "sudden stop," "bump in road," "landslides," etc. The red lines are warning signals that something important is coming up, that we must watch for it and determine by experience and discussion just exactly what type of evaluation and interpretation is required.

Along with the red-lining of the various musical segments, which indicates that this portion is important for the duration of the red line, we also, especially in the typical classic quartet, as well as in the majority of modern quartets, need delineation of the dynamic range in addition to the actual indicated dynamics. For instance, in the beginning *Allegro* of the first movement of the Mozart "Dissonant" Quartet, the first violin has a natural *crescendo* running through the first four measures, while the second violin and the viola have a *crescendo* and *decrescendo* in the third measure only, with the first violin *crescendo* continuing all the way through measure 9 (little *decrescendi* occurring within). It is also natural that the first violin would have a *crescendo* in measure 1 and a *decrescendo* to finish off the phrase in measure 2; then start again at measure 3 with a *crescendo* to measure 4 followed by a natural *decrescendo*. Measure 5 would have a slight *decrescendo* on the long-held note, then a *crescendo* for the last three eighth-notes of that measure where we have the finish of our phrase, then the final run through the completion of the *crescendo* until we reach the *forte* of measure 9.

I'm deliberately showing that there is more than one method of playing any group of notes. The point is that the mode of interpretation, which, in this particular example, is conceived by the first violin, can be determined by him in several different ways. No matter which way he chooses, the stressed red-line portions of the second violin and the viola (or any supporting part) remain the same. It is simply the degree and the direction that can change, and this is determined by the way the leading part is played. In this particular example, the first violin is playing the leading part. In other examples, the leader may be any of the other instruments, and whoever is the leader selects the interpretation that he wants, subject to the overall consensus of the quartet. When this is all put together, we have true ensemble playing. The stressed parts can be treated in different ways, but no matter how the leader interprets his part, these phrases will always be important and can be balanced to match with the leader's intentions.

After a quartet has been played a certain number of times, the red-line reminder will no longer be required. From that point on, the playing is almost automatic. Yet the red line will still serve a purpose, because it acts as a slight jolt, or tic, to the memory that something important is looming so that the interpretation of a string quartet will not have to rely so much on memorization of just what is or is not important—something which may require maybe thirty to one hundred performances before each individual player recalls exactly what he should be doing on almost every note and every phrase.

Red-lining, then, will make the whole business of playing quartets much simpler and clearer. The fact is that when you are playing a quartet seriously, there is an extraordinary amount of awareness demanded. Otherwise it's semi-automatic, and you'll miss a large percentage of the little ins and outs that differentiate the unpolished amateur from the accomplished professional. And, of course, our aim is to come as close to perfection as lies within our technical and musical abilities.

At this point we very strongly urge that the group purchase the scores, as mentioned earlier, for Mozart, Beethoven and Ravel—a total expenditure which is quite modest. It will be a lifetime investment that will pay for itself a thousand times over. For analysis and condensation of the learning process, this will be one of the prime requisites for anyone who takes his or her quartet playing seriously.

Analysis of these three quartets (the Mozart K 465 "Dissonant," the Beethoven Op. 59, No. 2 and the Ravel) forms the basis for analyzing the way to play all kinds of string quartets. For that reason, a portion of each of these three quartets will be analyzed in minutest detail. Patiently going through these quartets will more than compensate in the long run, because faithfully examining each quartet in so uncompromising a manner does more than give one an idea of how to play the particular composition, it gives one an idea of how to play any quartet in that style or period.

Now let us proceed to the preparations for the analysis of the string quartets chosen for this volume. The Mozart was selected because it represents the peak of so-called pure classicism; the Beethoven because it is by the great artist and creator of the finest classical romantic quartets; and the Ravel because it represents the apogee of the modern impressionistic "tone-color"-oriented string quartets.

First, the measures in each quartet should be numbered. As the manner of numbering differs somewhat for each of the three styles of quartet, we will cover this step as we get to each quartet. It will, however, be essential for ready reference, both when you set out to red-line your part and when, in playing, you have occasion to stop for discussion. Following this numbering step, you are ready to begin red-lining. The various levels of tone interpretation and indications of expression have been thoroughly discussed and the individual performer will, thanks to the red-line reminder, learn to fit his part in within a comparatively short time.

ACTUAL PLAYING

We now are ready to approach quartet playing itself on the instrumental level. The first axiom, which I will repeat countless times, is that we must remember and remember and remember: *No crunching,* no orchestral crackling, no symphonic attacks. This is definitely four soloists playing and you NEVER come down on the string with a whack of the bow. *Sforzandi* are done mostly with *vibrato* and a little more bow. Keep this in mind at all times. You will never hear a fine quartet give the *martelé* "crunch" of orchestral attack. This is absolutely *verboten* in string quartet playing.

Never forget that you are not *part* of a section; you are *the* section and, as such, a soloist on as high a level as anybody else in the ensemble. To my mind, it was only when a quartet such as the Guarneri got together four players, each on such a high level of perfection, that the string quartet as a form blossomed forth at its highest level and produced quartet music on a level I personally have never before experienced.

So, the three things to always keep in mind no matter what you are playing are: 1) no orchestral crunch; 2) no dead playing; you are one soloist among four, but still a soloist; 3) ensemble feeling—the realization that although each individual is playing a solo part, the complete or total effect can reach a musical level so high that it is no exaggeration to state that the highest level of musical realization can be produced by a superb performance of a masterwork by a master composer.

Before starting to play any quartet, the basics of tempo and bowing should be discussed and decided upon. For example, let us choose the tempo in the Scherzo movement of the Beethoven quartet that we are going to analyze later. In its basic skeletal structure, the rhythm and tempo of this particular movement are variegated. There are great variations in the tempo at which this movement is played. One can play it at a so-called concert tempo where it becomes a virtuosic display—approximately a metronome marking of 150 per quarter-note. At this tempo the rhythms become very complex, and the technique is much more on the "display" side and is more of a showpiece than anything else. But, on the contrary, quartets do play this movement at a much gentler tempo (the Guarneri, for instance) where they will play at closer to a 120 metronome marking. The movement itself will then take on a totally different character – much more gentle and without the virtuosic drive of the faster tempo.

Here is our basic problem: Which shall we choose or which characteristic are we aiming for? Allowing for the archetypal total ignorance of the quartet (that is to say, in the case where no one has ever played or heard the quartet), it is a problem that has to be solved according to the wishes of the players. There are several ways to work out the solution. The easiest one, of course, is to listen to a recording by one of the finer quartets (or, if possible, several recordings) and extract the essence of the tempos they would use in this movement which, again, can range from a gentle, easy tempo to a hard, driving virtuosic tempo. Still, the ensemble must keep in mind that the tempos they hear on a record are concert tempos, and so may not be really suitable for sightreading or may just be technically beyond the capacity of the quartet to play. However, listening to a record will give the players a very clear idea of what the piece should sound like, tempo being among the most basic of concerns.

Therefore, one way to find a tempo is to listen to a recording, see what the concert tempo is like, and then try to approach that concept which, if technically too difficult for the quartet, may be performed at a slower tempo than that on the record, but with the knowledge of all the performers that this is only for technical reasons, and that eventually they're going to work up to a tempo somewhere near that of the performance by a recognized fine quartet. Of course, this may work out the other way, too, such as the fact that a top group like the Guarneri plays the Scherzo a little slower than I have heard it played. In any case, listening to a recording is certainly one very secure way of acquiring an idea of tempo.

Now, turning to the opening Allegro of the Mozart "Dissonant" for a moment, we have the first violin playing a very flowing Mozartean melody somewhere between lush Brahms and somber Bach. One would therefore use a flowing type of bowing with no sharp changes of bow and no *staccato* accents and, in general, a more placid level of playing. Now, in contrast to this, second violin and viola are playing groups of eighth-notes as the accompaniment. It is up to the ensemble to decide whether they should play this accompaniment weakly, with a *staccato* type of *spiccato* or with a sharply outlined type of *staccato*. There are arguments for both ways. If they were to play with the more fluid type of *staccato*, we would get more of a blend with the lead theme. On the contrary, if they played with a sharp *spiccato*, accented every measure or even every second beat, we would get more of a contrast with the flowing output of the first violin. This is simply one example of how bowings are determined by the type of music that the ensemble wishes to produce.

The third base on which a lovely ensemble tone is perfected is the use of *vibrato*. In fact, in the final analysis, the *vibrato* can be *the* most important factor in determining the quality and type of the ensemble tone. Our axiom here is that, except in the most ethereal, triple *pianissimo*, crystal-like chords, *vibrato* is used in all its infinite varieties by all four players. By using *vibrato* judiciously, yet constantly, the tone never falls dead. Also, the richness of the tonal output is magnified many times by the use of a rich *vibrato*, especially in the inner parts. As the players acquaint themselves more and more with quartet playing and any quartet in particular, they will soon realize that it is the inner parts that supply the richness and variety of tone that makes the quartet into an artistic masterpiece. Conversely, the first violin or cello or anyone can play his heart out vibrating like crazy on some theme or solo and, if the others don't help him out with similar rich types of *vibrato*, his playing will not melt into the group, but on the contrary will stick out like the proverbial sore thumb.

WARMING UP

The first basic thing is to get a concept of playing together and playing in tune. What I suggest is to choose a couple of simple eight bar phrases, such as those which start out the second movement of the "Death and the Maiden" quartet by Schubert, and play it in the following manner:

First—led by the first violin, an ethereal double *piano* with everybody listening with the most acute attention and all trying to play with the same quality of tone and with the most perfect intonation possible.

Next—let the second violin lead, and we can choose all kinds of ways to play it. Let's say, for instance, we play these first two refrains double *forte marcato*, but again listening very carefully to play in tune and play together.

Thus, we go on, with the viola, let's say, leading a double *piano* with a tremendous *crescendo* and back down to double *piano*.

And the cello—very, very smooth *mezzo forte* with sudden *ritardandi* and variations in tone production up and down with all the rest listening with all their might and trying to play together, so that the total effect is *one*.

When this has been done—when you have gone through the gamut of having each take turns leading with all types of playing attempted—the quartet is ready to start with Mozart, Haydn, or anything else. This way you don't waste the first twenty minutes sort of learning to play together and learning to play in tune. You've worked it out in the simplicity of the Schubert, and since it is done every time the group meets, the various harmonies are well known and recognizable, so that if the micro-second something is not correct, it is immediately apparent to the entire quartet. This makes it that much easier to correct and to get the whole idea in your mind.

Another way of selecting a tempo for any movement is by attempting to follow the metronome markings with which a great deal of music is inflicted. When one considers that 90% of all these metronome markings have been inserted by some editor who was influenced by a friend or a performance he had heard maybe in 1850 or 1890, the reader will recognize that these metronome markings can be and are quite misleading. I, for one, do not pay much attention to the metronome markings and use them only as a last resort when nobody actually knows what the quartet should sound like and there's no record available and the players have to grope for a correct tempo.

Using one of these three methods, then—experience of a listener or a performer, a record of a good quartet, or a metronome marking—will finally give a very good idea of the tempo in which the quartet should be played.

Usually, the most competent musician in the group (more often the first violin) selects a tempo on the basis of the above criteria, which launches the quartet. Within a few bars there will be cries of "Too fast for me!" and various other objections, after which the tempo will be adjusted to the point where everybody can manage his part adequately or at least with enough ease to make the quartet play. On the other hand, many players who are not technically in the upper echelon will complain that if the tempo is slowed down too much, certain bowings become ten times as hard to play as at a faster tempo and, furthermore, at too slow a tempo one does not get the sense of the music that one is playing. So what the Saturday-night players end up with is a compromise between the technical level of the best player and that of the least skilled player, yet at the same time keeping the tempo going fast enough so that the sense of the music is not lost.

The other basic determination in string quartet playing is exactly what kind of bowings to use and where. There are a number of factors to be considered here. Let us start with the most obvious and simplest and work our way as deeply and to as much complexity as we can accomplish.

There are two axioms of which all quartet players should be aware, if they are not already so. One is that, in playing Haydn quartets, ninety percent of all the bowing is *on* the string; in playing Mozart quartets, ninety per cent of all the bowing is *spiccato*, whenever the opportunity offers itself. Beethoven would be a combination of the two, as would Brahms. Using these four composers as the foundation on which to build our understanding of how to play all quartets, these axioms will serve as the vehicle on which to base most of your bowings. The axioms just quoted will cover most of the bowings in the classic quartets that are performed.

Difficulties arise when you concern yourself with matching the bowings of one player with those of another. First, let us dispose of the illusion that unanimity of bowing, such as everybody playing down bow or up bow at the same time, contributes something to the ensemble as a whole. Mechanically, it may, but musically and in every other way, it serves no valid purpose. We must realize that we are not four components all playing the same orchestral part, but instead tend more to be four individual soloists, each with his own likes and dislikes. And if the effects desired can be achieved by the first violin playing up bow and the second violin playing down bow on similar notes or phrases, this is actually to be preferred.

Bowings are used in a much more subtle manner than in larger ensembles or even in solo playing. The inner parts can, for instance, maintain their volume at the level desired, yet at the same time, by using more or less bow, accenting with the bow, playing the bow on different parts of the string, they can achieve numerous tonal effects which will contribute very much to the artistic level of the ensemble.

The other advantage of weighing what bowing to use is that the use of the bow in certain ways will allow the parts to merge or be differentiated in a much clearer manner.

One of the last authentic portraits of the divine Mozart.

RED-LINE ANALYSIS OF MOZART "DISSONANT" QUARTET K. 465, FIRST MOVEMENT

A few more general remarks should be made before we start on the actual evaluation. One is that, for various reasons, dynamics are usually indicated on the most primitive level. This may be for as simple and obvious a reason as that the editor or composer is simply too lazy to mark one part *mp* and the next part *p* and the next part *mf*, and so on. In working out the quartet, the level of dynamics should be determined by the importance of the particular part the instrument is playing. Also various modes of emphasis must be added in the form of dynamics so that the music doesn't become some kind of formless mass with an obvious solo jutting out—the whole adding up to little more than nothing.

In the three quartets under discussion, we are going to be scrupulously detailed, especially in the introduction to the Mozart, which happens to have more subtle changes and nuances, more things for each individual player to watch and do in this little introduction, than there are in the rest of the first movement and probably in the rest of the entire quartet.

In this Mozart introduction, the cello starts out with straightforward eighth-notes marked *piano*. In order to give pace to the quartet—to get it off its feet and set it in motion—he cannot commence playing softly out of nowhere.

The entrance could be indicated by a slight accent on the first note with an abrupt *diminuendo,* accomplished by a quick vibrato with a pulse immediately setting the rhythm and then fading out within the space of an eighth–note into the simple beat that the cello is initiating. On the third beat of that measure the viola comes in with a rather strange note, also marked *piano.* But this is definitely a solo *piano* and should again have a vibrato accent with a quick *diminuendo.*

We should now refer to the fact that the dynamics are determined by the mood of the composition and are confirmed by the opening cello lead.

One warning which will be repeated over and over again is that in quartet performance there must be no crunching, no crackling, no harsh attacks. Ninety-eight per cent of all the playing is done very subtly with the bow and, even more important, with vibrato, vibrato accents, vibrato *crescendi, decrescendi* and all the other resources the instrument is able to command.

Returning to the third beat of measure 1 of the introduction, the viola definitely enters as a solo instrument. Put a red line under the first note which would immediately *decrescendo* so that, in measure 2, the second violin can bring out his E-flat marked by the red line and a vibrato accent which drops abruptly to give the first violin, in measure 2, the opportunity to red-line his A-natural so that we get the effect we seek. Although we have had these solo entrances through measure 2, from the time the viola has entered, his is a solo part and should be played as such, especially the leading F-sharp third quarter-note of the second measure, so that when we reach measure 3, where the first and second violin play the first two quarter-notes, the viola actually finishes up the last three eighth-notes as a definite solo with solo vibrato and solo tone.

At the same time, we can't forget that the last eighth-note of the second measure is reinforced by the second violin part which repeats the motif of the four ascending notes that the viola has just played. The moment the second violin finishes, the first violin repeats the motif of the ascending four-note scale. Now there is a slight addition: as the first violin finishes these first four bars, he is reinforced by the cello who also plays notes in an ascending scale phrase and dynamically is at least equal to the first violin.

In measure 5, as the first violin finishes his phrase, the cello starts over again.

Measures 5 through 8 are interpreted in the same manner as the first four measures.

At measure 9 we have a duet between the second violin and viola. Both phrases would receive red-lines through measures 9 and 10, except that in measure 10, when the second violin plays his E-flat, he pulls the dynamics down a bit to allow the viola to finish up his phrase with the four-note ascending scale which has been declared ever since measure 3.

In measure 11, the viola has a dotted half-note which obviously, after the initial attack, is background, so this should be played as a finish to the four-note phrase, which is solo *piano*. The four-note phrase is red-lined and then fades out into the background.

Also in measure 11, the first violin enters with the primary theme of the introduction, but again we must keep in mind that at the same time the first violin enters on the second eighth-note of the bar, the second violin interjects two sixteenth-notes and a half-note. Following these three notes — F, E-flat and D, the second violin abruptly fades out so that the counter theme to the first violin's primary melody will not be lost.

As the first violin finishes his phrase with a high G in measure 12, he makes his immediate *decrescendo* (not *too* sudden, because it *is* the melody and we don't want it to vanish into limbo), leaving dynamic room for the second violin and viola to bring out their interweaving parts, which together make a beautiful whole. We return to the last three eighth-notes in the first violin in measure 12 where once again we have the motif of the four ascending notes repeated and red-lined by the second violin in measure 13, where, together with the second violin, the cello plays an equally important part with his ascending chromatic scale.

The moment the cello reaches the first beat of measure 14, he, together with the viola and first violin, lowers his dynamics a trifle so that the chromatic solo of the second violin may be stressed as it goes into measure 15. Here again we have, at measure 14, one of the finest examples of Mozart scoring. Each of the four parts is vital to the music. The first violin has a descending chromatic motif in quarter-notes. At the same time the second violin is playing a chromatic scale in eighth-notes, while the last three eighth-notes of the measure are played by the cello who blends with the second and the first violin. Just as they finish on the first beat of measure 15, the upbeat of a rising scale motif is played by the viola, who, against all this harmonic competition must rise to the occasion with a definite solo not to be lost in the musical matrix.

However, in measure 15, the first violin continues with his solo when he makes the turn in sixteenth-notes for the last six notes of the measure. Do not forget that in measure 15 the cello has a very important second quarter-note where he flats the note and changes the harmony completely. When he plays this flatted note, it definitely calls for a stress of some kind, whether it be vibrato or more bow, but without increasing the volume.

Measure 16 seems to indicate that it could be the end of the introduction, but Mozart is not quite through. We have a *sforzando* note played by the cello where, again, we can give a solo vibrato to the *sf* (and a cadence of eighth-notes) to finish that measure.

This presentation is repeated in measures 17 and 18. Then in measure 19 the cello becomes quite prominent and begins to conclude the introduction with repeated eighth-notes. On the third eighth-note, as the first and second violin are playing quiet eighths, the viola and cello have a *sforzando* marked on the second half of the second quarter which should be brought out with an artistic vibrato accent.

Now the first and second violin reply in measure 20 with a *sforzando vibrato* accent on their first eighth-note, at which point they quickly fade back to *piano*. Along come the cello and viola and repeat the same type of performance as in measure 19 and on into measure 21.

We end up with a *vibrato fp* indicated for all parts except the first violin, who is playing a superlative solo, concluding with full *vibrato solo* interpretation and a cadenza type of playing as the soloist and leader.

I want to point out that almost twenty minutes has been spent in tearing apart these few lines of introductory Adagio. The reader, especially the so-called "amateur," will, of course, ask, "Is all this necessary? Isn't this going too deeply just to enjoy an evening's entertainment? Haven't we gotten together more to learn the literature, to experience a new quartet? Why do you find it so profoundly needful to tear to pieces an introduction (admittedly, in the immortal category), dealing with it at the deepest level of quartet playing?"

I can only answer by saying that in going through these three quartets as examples, they will be analyzed to the smallest detail NOT for the sake of performance or for getting to learn the quartet so well that every single note has its place and each performer knows exactly what to do at what time, in what way, and in what manner. Rather, it is that, after these three different types of quartets are covered thoroughly, the player will, from that time on, be able to play any type of quartet and have a good idea of exactly what importance his part plays in the performance of the quartet and what he himself should and must do to make the quartet into a work of art such as all quartet players are seeking to accomplish.

Therefore, please drudge your way through this detailed analysis, keeping in the back of your mind that this is the bread-and-butter of how to play quartets. The reason for being so thorough in the analysis is so that from now on a quartet will not be a sort of semi-mystery or a series of connected or disconnected phrases which the individual player doesn't quite know how to handle, except to let the first violin play havoc with, or make a concerto out of, the quartet. Instead, you will be given a very solid idea of where your place is in the quartet structure along with a very clear idea of how you should play your part, what type of phrase, run, note or harmony to stress, what kind of tone level and quality to use at various points in the quartet. In a word, hammering away at understanding every smallest detail of these three quartets will give you a profound conception of what to do with any quartet you may come across.

Now to the Allegro. The construction of this section is relatively simple. The first violin is playing the theme.

In measure 1 of the Allegro, the last three eighth-notes should be stressed by the second violin to blend with the first. In measure 3 we have a duet by the second violin and viola which should be stressed a little; in this case, by opening the second quarter with a slight vibrato and then quickly diminuendoing so that the first violin can continue his solo. In measure 4 the second violin, after the initial eighth-note, has a stress on the rest of the measure.

Measure 5 is a repetition of measure 3 and should be played in the same manner. Measure 6 has interesting chromatic turns by second violin and viola which should be stressed, although at all times this is definitely a first violin solo. In fact, the second violin and viola run through measures 6 and 7 with a very interesting descending figure which ends in measure 7 with two leading tones by the viola that should sound; keep in mind, still, that the first violin is at all times playing the solo. These stresses that have been indicated for the second violin and viola are simply ways and means for keeping the *obbligato* interesting and adding energy to the presentation of the quartet.

As we come to measure 9 we now have the original allegro theme presented *forte,* and accompanying figurations are much more elaborate. At the end of measure 9, the second violin should not get lost. His eighth-notes should be on a par with, and blend equally with, the first violin.

At measure 10 we have a solo entrance by the cello followed by a solo entrance by the viola. This is repeated in measure 11 by the violins. In measure 12, the cello once again gives us some important eighth-notes followed by the viola at a solo level, finishing up with a *sforzando.*

In measure 14 we again have to watch that, although marked *sf* this is not an orchestral *sf* but a tight vibrato with a little extra bow. It's a *sf* within a *piano.*

In measure 16 the same pattern that has been going on through the Allegro continues. The solo is definitely the first, yet there is a counter *obbligato* by the second violin and viola which carries through to measure 18. At measure 18 the pattern and duration of quarter-notes which have been set by the cello back in measure 16 are now joined in by the second and viola. As the cello in measure 16 starts drawing long, breathy, smooth quarters, when 18 is reached all three of the accompanying instruments should draw the same kind of quarter-notes.

This pattern continues to measure 21 where we encounter the next *forte* with an emotional *obbligato* by the viola for the second, third, and fourth quarter-notes and a descending stress and blending with the first violin to finish up that measure with the entire pattern resolving in measure 22.

These few measures that have been analyzed as to redlines, stresses and leadership are intended to serve as a model for the rest of the movement.

We have established by this detailed analysis of the Mozart quartet that there are no such things as static bars,

David Soyer plays his cello part for the other members of the Quartet.

phrases or melodies. All that this detailed analysis amounts to is, as soon as one part starts playing a note of some duration without change, whether it be melody or *obbligato*, some other part is propelling the quartet forward with some type of motion—be it a group of eighth-notes, a change in rhythm, a change in tone volume (i.e., *crescendo* and *decrescendo*), or even a change in harmony where a leading tone, or some other dissonant tone, is injected for interest and helps carry forward the progression of the theme.

This outlook towards quartet playing will serve to give an idea of what parts to bring out, when to sink back, and, in the long run and finally, the whole concept will become almost automatic. In a quartet such as the Mozart quartet whose introduction we just covered in detail, and where you will find few printed instructions (*piano, forte, crescendo, decrescendo*, and so forth), the style and method of playing the quartet itself can be easily determined by applying this type of outlook to the construction of the quartet itself.

This portrait of the middle-aged Beethoven succeeds in conveying some of his strength of character.

RED-LINE ANALYSIS OF BEETHOVEN OP. 59, NO. 2

Introduction

As was done with the introduction of the Mozart quartet, the major part of the Beethoven first movement will be dissected in great detail. It will be very worthwhile to the sometime quartet player (non-professional) to study in detail a work such as this particular Beethoven. Then the lessons learned can be applied to all music because the principle is exactly the same and can be expressed in very few words.

There may be one leading voice or all may be combined – that is, one to four leading voices; there can be a counter melody; there could be a harmonic *obbligato*; there could be a tremendous amount of voice leading and tone stressing. All of this can be covered by red-lining (that is, underlining in red) the particular phrase, note and solo – things which we have gone through before.

Now, using this principle of stressing a part that is impor-tant to the continuity or the harmony of the quartet, any quar-tet can be played using these principles. Furthermore, if these principles are observed, by the time a quartet is played twice it will sound like a piece of music and not a jumble of silences, disharmonies, blanks, and dead spots. There will always be something important going on.

And finally, the more each little phrase is stressed in the right place at the right time with the correct volume, the correct balance, the closer and closer one will get to realizing a performance in the grand manner—that is, approaching the standards of the finest professional quartets.

FIRST MOVEMENT

The Mozart quartet we just analyzed is undoubtedly one of the finest quartets ever written. Emotionally, the "Dissonant" introduction to the first movement is as deeply moving and full of passion as any music ever composed. However, the introduction is a very small portion of the quartet, and the rest of the work is typical Mozart—glorious combinations of tones, rhythms, harmonies, wonderful development of sections, all laid over with the patina of Mozart's genius. Still, we must remind ourselves that, outside of that one incredible introduction, the emotional range is still eighteenth-century and we don't have what one would call real depth of emotion or the deeper philosophical type of music. It must also be mentioned that Mozart did write some wonderfully passionate music in his operas but, though we are aware of that, this particular quartet was deliberately selected in order to compare it to the quartet we are coming to, the Op. 59, No. 2 of Beethoven.

Beethoven was the great creator of all the passions in music. He wrote music in rage, in protest, in poignant expression of melancholy, in unbearable stretching of the emotions. His music is on a deeper philosophical level than that of all previous composers, except Bach and Händel, who, having come years earlier, do not pertain to our present investigation.

It is this emotional range that Beethoven carried forward in such quartets as the Op. 59, No. 2 which we now want to explore. As a matter of fact, Op. 59, No. 2 forms a dividing line. Op. 59, No. 1 has still more or less the fluent beauty and the matchless skill of a Beethoven development and does not delve too deeply into the stronger emotions. Op. 59, No. 2, although more complex and difficult to play and understand, provides what I consider the quartet exemplar of Beethoven at this tragic peak. The mood of Op. 59, No. 2 is cast in the same mold as that of the *Eroica* Symphony. Although four creation-filled years separate them, we can account for their similarity by the fact that they are ground-breakers for their particular medium within Beethoven's second period into which he was catapulted by the onslaught of deafness.

The quartet opens with two tragic chords in the manner of the second measure of the *Egmont* Overture. The chords are each of two eighth-notes duration followed by an eighth-note rest in a 6/8 measure and are marked with a *staccato* dot. Care should be taken not to chop off the chords and make them too *sec*, and yet, as they are deliberately marked with dots, one should not make the chords too broad. A good way to play these chords (which set the mood for the entire movement) is with a lot of bow and strictly in time, making sure the duration does not overlap the rests; then, after the bow is withdrawn from the strings, the vibrato should continue so that the chords ring out. Now the measure rest should be silently counted by each player and a *double piano, misterioso* motif enters, played by violin and cello. Another measure rest follows, and the pattern is repeated *misterioso, double piano*. Care should be taken that the chords are resolved mainly in the second violin and viola.

The ninth measure has an unusual expression marking in the viola which can be played very successfully using the following technique: finger the triplet 2, 1, 3. When going from 1 to 3 you slide up on the first finger and then slap the string with the third finger to give you your *sfz* without any crunch of the box; then a quick *vibrato* and fade, as immediately afterwards the first violin enters with the same type of phrase.

Measure 10 resolves in the second violin.

In measure 11 the same motif is repeated by first and second violins where we use the fingering 3, 1, 3 both in the first and the second violins in the same manner as in the previous two measures, answered by the cello using the same fingering with upward slide of the first finger and slap of the third finger, then a quick vibrato and right down.

Now the first main theme enters in the first violin, *piano*, *crescendo*, in a tragic, almost tearful, manner. As he finishes the first four notes, ending on a D-sharp, the sixteenth-notes must be clearly outlined in the second violin and viola.

The next measure repeats the idea once more, and the same answers should be observed. As we go on to the next measure, we have the running sixteenth-notes which follow on in this key until at measure 18 we culminate in a *crescendo*.

Keep in mind that, until this measure, we have been playing in the *piano* range at all times. One of the greatest things in this first movement, and one of the things to especially watch for, is that some of the most dramatic moments occur while the volume is *piano*, and particular attention should be paid to this fact, so that when the *crescendo* finally comes (as it does now) it will be that much more dramatic. The *crescendo* at measure 18 leads us back into the opening tragic, grandiose chords, differently harmonized and spaced but played in the original manner.

After a measure rest we reach measure 21 where careful counting lets the second violin bring in his sixteenths, answered by the viola sixteenth-notes, while the first violin is playing a group of notes which are not quite a melody but rather a counter melody to what the second violin and viola are doing. This type of playing goes on for several measures when the unison and octave runs start again.

Now the *crescendo* runs up into a double *forte*. When it reaches the top of the double *forte*, care should especially be taken to mark the last two sixteenth-notes very hard and dry, so that the double *forte* itself will stand out as the top of the climax. Also, it will clarify the sixteenth-notes which the three lower instruments are now playing.

In the last eighth-note of this measure, a trill by the first violin leads into a rising *arpeggio* which should be brilliantly played while the rest of the quartet are doing *sforzandi* on the downbeat. The execution of all the passages through this part is fairly clear. However, what we are now looking for is emotion. Beethoven is raging from one climax to another and it should be played in that way. When the first violin comes to the top of his passage, the two sixteenth-notes against the trills of the second violin and viola should be emphasized.

The *sforzando* of measure 28 should really be a blow by all four participants. This pattern is repeated for several more measures, after which the counterpoint weaves in and out and finally ends at measure 33 with four very dramatically executed *staccato* eighth-notes. One of the things to watch carefully is that in the two bars before measure 33, the cello ends each bar with three sixteenth-notes. These notes should be stressed and not lost in the shuffle. The emphatic execution of these notes will add much to the dramatic impact of the passage.

At measure 33 we end the first dramatic surge and *decrescendo* in the viola to a new theme where the cello is now playing a fluent, rising melody answered by a lovely passage in the first violin. The cello repeats the same type of passage and is answered, again, in the next measure by the first violin who plays a passage of Beethovenian lyricism extending for three measures.

In measure 40 we have a ticklish little phrasing where the last three sixteenth-notes are shared by the first violin, second violin, and cello. Again, the cello especially should not let his part be overshadowed by the others. Be sure of the rhythm. Balance the tone level so that it is not lost in the overall ensemble.

In the next measure the second violin is now playing the primary melody with the rest of the instruments coming in with sixteenth-notes at different times. These must be kept prominent. Don't let them be submerged in the overall harmony.

In measure 43, the solo, or the melody, is now shared by three instruments. The way to play this is: while the first violin is playing his lovely long note, the second violin should stress his sixteenth-notes even though they are marked *dolce*; then, as the first violin ends up the measure with a group of sixteenth-notes, we have the same problem. The last four sixteenth-notes are shared by the first violin, second violin and viola. From here until measure 49, the playing is all straightforward. The sixteenth-notes should be brought out, not lost in the shuffle. Therefore they should be red-lined to remind the individual players of their importance.

At measure 47, the second violin, viola, and cello should play warm, long notes as the first violin displays his sixteenth-note figurations. A vibrato accent on each of the long notes would not be amiss at this point.

Then at measure 48, we have a rich *crescendo* with everybody vibrating—their single notes blending together in a chordlike fashion—as we come into measure 49.

Measure 49 is one of the dramatic highlights. Now it seems as if Beethoven is almost in a frenzy. The music should be played with passionate emphasis. A good way to play this passage, and one that will make it very effective, is to hold the dotted eighth as long as possible, but strictly within rhythm; the sixteenth-notes at the frog; the *sforzandi* on the dotted eighths specially singled out and played very dramatically by the use of a throbbing *vibrato*. Suddenly, at the third measure after 49, there is a quick *decrescendo* to a *piano dolce*, which is led by the viola for two measures. Then the dramatic episode initiated at measure 49 repeats itself and, again, we have this *decrescendo* to a *piano*.

At measure 57, the melody is taken up by the first violin, who plays his cadenza-like passage in sixteenth-notes, at the same time backing down to a double *piano*.

Here we enter a region of off-beats which, although double *piano*, should be made very dramatic by the use of a tiny touch of a *marcato* separation of each note plus a hint of a *vibrato* accent on each note change. Then, where the *crescendo* is printed (it should be recalled that this is all in *pp*), hold back the increasing volume as long as possible. The real crescendo doesn't start until it is marked *più crescendo* and then we rise to the culminating *forte* where, at four bars before the first ending, everyone is playing with great rhythmic virility.

A special suggestion here for the first violin is to play his sixteenth-notes all up bow, near the frog. In this way he can get a tremendously effective *marcato*—biting, accented tone —and conclude with one of the most dramatic finishes to an opening movement's exposition section that we will ever hear in a string quartet.

Going on to the second section, we have more of the same and this leads us back to the original dramatic "Egmont" chords. Don't forget to use lots of bow, broad but not too broad, short but not too short, and vibrate after the note is played. Suddenly, after the silent six-beat count, the same type of chord changes to a *piano* and, after another measure rest, to a double *piano*. What should be kept in mind here is that this is not simply a question of lessening the volume. You want to put as much feeling into the chords as if they were double *forte*.

After another measure rest, we suddenly jump back to double *forte* chords, with the first violin holding a vibrant F-sharp for a full measure, whereupon the cello enters with his three eighth-notes. The resolution of the second violin and viola concludes the phrase as the first violin renders his group of deeply-felt sixteenth-notes.

After a measure rest, at measure 81 the same pattern is repeated. The cello enters with a beautiful solo tone along with a partial resolution led by the second violin. We go on to a new type of melody which, at first, is very placid and lucid with eighth-notes in the first violin answered by the eighths in cello; then sixteenths answered by sixteenths. This type of writing continues and becomes more and more dramatic in a plaintive sort of fashion.

At measure 88 we have a continuation of the original theme in the first violin with everyone else repeating one of the original motifs. Thus, we finally come to measure 91 which, at first glance, seems to be the same type of off-beats that we have played in the exposition but a closer look shows that this is different — slightly, but still not the same. In this case, the first and second violins are playing off-beats. They are not the *marcato* type, separated off-beats, but rather very smooth — to be played with a beautiful *vibrato* and tone. While this is going on for four measures, the viola and cello are playing eighth-notes (separated by eighth-rests) between the top two instruments' beats and changes of bowing or changes of notes, giving an entirely different effect than that of its earlier parallel.

A *crescendo* quickly starts and rises to a dramatic *forte* and then, just as dramatically, the music falls off to a sudden *piano* where we have one of the previous motifs repeated with the first violin playing ornamentations against the main melody which is shared by the second violin and viola. It should be emphasized that this is a typical situation now developing — one which seems to have been initiated, in large measure, by Beethoven. We are leaving the type of quartet music which has one or two leading players, usually the first violin and cello, who play their melodies and are accompanied by the inner parts. This is no longer so. All three (or four) parts are vital and should be played with a solo tone and stressed. The only thing to be worked out (outside of the actual notes) is just how much weight should be given to each part.

In the last two measures we discussed, it seems the parts are about equally balanced. The second violin and viola are playing a reminiscence of previous themes, while the first violin has beautiful broken *arpeggi* offering sterling opportunities for emotional artistry (although, still, the entire passage is held down to a *piano* level). We now re-enter the previous type of playing with the first and second violin playing smooth off-beats while the viola and cello are playing their notes in between with just a little *vibrato* so that all four instruments are slightly separated. It is not a purely *legato* form of playing, but should be clearly delineated. Then we get what we are seeking – a disturbing off-beat effect – and, again, dramatic music that is Beethoven at his best.

We continue holding back on the *crescendo* and finally rising to our double *forte* at measure 107 where the first and second violins play as virtuoso soloists – very broad strokes and double *forte*. They are joined by the viola continuing in the same manner and then by the cello which, by now, is playing in thirds with the viola. As they finish their passage, the first and second violins come in again and play the same type of tremendously dramatic bowing, again joined by the viola and then the paired viola and cello.

All this has been going on since measure 49 at top volume.

Here, again, at measure 115 we have a precipitous drop to a double *piano*, where the plaintive original melody is played by the first violin and joined by the second. Whenever this theme is played, the second violin has to be especially careful not to lose his last three sixteenth-notes in that measure, but rather to bring them out. This is definitely a duet situation. Both instruments are equally important and the duet should be played with equally luscious (or plaintive, or whatever the emotional makeup calls for) solo-quality tone.

Now we go on to repeat what has been done before – the same types of runs and the same types of *arpeggi* that we have had thus far – until we reach measure 133 where we have a different style of emphasizing the notes by having all four instruments play trills in double *forte*. The only thing to watch in measure 133 is that the second violin and viola have a double *forte sfz* on the second eighth-note of the measure. This provides a tremendous impact and should not be overlooked.

Measure 139 has similar groups of sixteenth-notes repeated: first violin, viola; first violin and second violin together; viola (emphatically though still *piano*); cello (*subito fortissimo*); back to viola; first violin; cello (with authority, but *piano*). We are back to the original opening melody, double *piano*. In fact, from here until measure 183 it is a repetition of the opening page with all the same dynamics and observing the same intensity of the various parts.

At measure 183 the second violin should stress his part quite strongly to bring it out clearly against the first violin who is playing the solo. We have here the same problem — the last three or four sixteenth-notes are shared by three instruments and care should be taken to play these together as clearly and perfectly as possible.

At measure 184 the cello has the counter lead in sixteenth-notes answered by the first violin. While he finishes, both the second violin and viola have sixteenth-notes which they should stress. In the second half of measure 185, three sixteenth-notes are played by the first violin and cello while the last three sixteenth-notes are played by all four instruments. No note should be lost in the clamor. All are equally important. In fact, as a general rule, in most quartets, to keep the quartet in motion musically, whoever has a part that is a smaller division of the time interval than the others is usually either playing the lead or a very important counter melody, and his subdivided time intervals should be stressed.

As is typical in sonata form, measures 189 ff. are a repetition of what has previously occurred, as are measures 205 ff. However, in measure 207 there is a crucial viola solo which should be brought out with all possible power because, since everybody else is playing *sfz forte*, he will have a very tough time making his part heard. The same is true of the next measure.

Now, as we approach the coda, the notes themselves are rather simple. Whichever instrument is in motion, whoever plays more notes in the beat than his companions, has the lead. We repeat once more the off-beat type of syncopation where the first and second violins are playing *legato* eighths with the viola and cello eighths falling between, with care being taken to hold it down, hold it down, double *piano*, and to hold back the *crescendo*. Finally, in measure 237, we reach a tremendous climax—the climax of the whole first movement—where the first and second violins play dramatic chords answered by a double *forte* throb of the viola and cello, forming a dominant flatted-ninth chord. First and second violin again. Viola and cello again. A quick, smooth *decrescendo* through the next measure, at which point the first violin rounds off the whole passage with the sixteenth-note figuration we have heard several times before, and we are back into the original plaintive theme. All the previous effects are now repeated. We have a few *crescendi* which even work up to a double *forte* five bars from the end, but then die out, *diminuendo*, and, after all the storm and turmoil, we end with three perfectly placed E minor chords.

ADAGIO

The suggestions for the first movement can now be carried out in the Adagio movement using all the methods that have been discussed and analyzed up to this point. There should be no unusual difficulties that will cause any hesitancy on the part of the players in putting forth their best and most beautiful efforts and, in so doing, produce an extraordinary movement. There is nothing unusual in this movement that would need any special analysis, since we've already covered enough examples to make the performance of the movement clear and definitive. Now, to the allegretto Scherzo.

SCHERZO

For some reason, this Scherzo offers unusual rhythmic

patterns which seem to upset many performers. I have played in many quartets which, after ten or twelve measures, simply bog down and cannot perform the movement.

The solution is very simple. It is just that the cello should emphasize his first beat with very firm authority, almost an accent, even though the whole thing is double *piano*. If he performs in this manner, and the first violin makes sure that, especially during the first couple of performances, he plays his part very, very rhythmically and precisely, everything will fall into place and the movement will become the rhythmically very simple pattern that it actually consists of.

The effect on the listener may sound quite complex, but when the quartet is analyzed and performed in this manner, it becomes quite a simple movement for the players. Later on, the subtleties — little *crescendi*, greater or lesser accents, bringing out various parts and various parts of the harmonies — can be explored and the beauty of the movement enhanced more and more until, ultimately, it becomes the incredible Scherzo — one of the finest Beethoven ever wrote.

One more thing about this Scherzo is the fact that, contrary to what one might think, playing it faster and faster does not make it more rhythmical. The Guarneri Quartet, for instance, plays it quite slowly, but the slower tempo allows them to bring out the subtleties much more and the players do not get lost in a welter of fast notes and slurred rhythmic phrasing.

TRIO

The Trio is very straightforward. Everything is very plainly marked. There are no subtleties that I can see. The whole thing consists simply of various renderings of the theme in different combinations of first violin and cello, second violin and viola . . . in fact, all the possible combinations, and works itself up to a tremendous double *forte* climax, going down to the repetition of the original theme.

FINALE

And so we finish up with the Presto which, again, is very straightforward and is more of a virtuoso presentation by the first violin than is usual in Beethoven's quartets. One type of phrasing might be applied to this quartet for emphasis. As you see, the word "might" is used because the players can think of dozens of ways to enhance the quartet. The middle part can be played more or less accented. Different types of bowing may be used by the inner parts and by varying the way the inner parts are played. By playing every repetition of the background for the primary melody in a slightly different manner, the musical interest can be kept at a high level. Primarily, of course, since it is a virtuoso display, in this movement it is really up to the first violin to display the utmost bravura and virtuosity in his presentation of the entire movement. The movement thus proceeds until it culminates in a peak of excitement.

Ravel was one of the most esthetically refined and sensuous composers of his generation.

RED-LINE ANALYSIS OF RAVEL QUARTET

Finally we come to the Ravel String Quartet, which I consider to be the finest example of modern tone-painting and impressionism ever written for string quartet.

FIRST MOVEMENT

This quartet commences with a simple, almost country air in the first violin which works up to a natural peak in the first four measures. However, the simplicity is modified by a scale in tenths played by the second violin and cello which crescendos along with the first violin until he reaches his top C which is the peak of that four-measure phrase. Immediately on the third beat of that measure where the first violin reaches his peak, the second violin plays the third and fourth beat (which should be red-lined) as an answer to the first violin and this completes the four measure phrase.

In this Ravel quartet, the interweaving of the parts is only part of the tonal magic evoked in the composition. What we are going to concentrate on in this analysis is the way different qualities of tone and different types of harmonies are built up and utilized so that we enter a new realm of harmonic wizardry. From the start of the composition, the use of passing tones and other modern devices creates a type of harmony that has left nineteenth-century and all previous tonalities far behind. Although we don't want to go to the trouble of analyzing each note, it is enough to know that the so-called strange, modern harmonies are generated more by the use of passing tones than by utilizing other devices.

The second phrase, lasting from measures 5 through 8, again is led by a simple melody played by the first violin. Here the thing to watch is that the eighth-notes that are inserted not only carry the theme along, but help create the imagery and the harmonic originality that Ravel was aiming for. In this case, at measure 5, the viola has the first three eighth-notes red-lined, so that, as the first violin is playing his simple melody, the viola is already inserting his eighth-notes to continue the line which started in the first violin and went to the second, and which goes from the viola back to the first violin.

In measure 8, while the first violin holds his last quarter-note over into the first beat of the measure, the three other instruments change notes and harmonies and thus need to stress their first note. If one will look at the score, one will notice that Ravel himself put a broad line on the first beat of the first violin's held-over note. Since measure 8 is at the top of the *crescendo* for all four instruments and a broad stress line is indicated for the first violin, the latter increases the emphasis by adding a *vibrato* on the first eighth-note of that eighth measure, while the others also stress their change of note with a little extra *vibrato*. They too are at the top of the crescendo which then fades out in all four instruments with the natural ending in the first violin. With measure 8, we now have a very subtle stress in the viola part where lie the only moving notes in beats three and four ending the phrase, so we red-line quarter-notes three and four for the viola.

Going forward, we switch to two-bar phrases. Although the prime melody is in the first violin for two bars, it is then answered by the second violin in the next two bars. Then, in bar 13, we switch to one-bar phrases and in this case the first and second violins play a phrase in even quarter-notes while the viola and cello are playing half-notes which are

112

very important in bringing out the Ravelian harmony. The lines are marked by Ravel himself. The only thing we can add is that we might as well red-line it to remind the players that, besides the fact that the harmony is unusual, a *vibrato* of beauty should be used; don't let the notes die. We have the *crescendo* coming up, and the one-bar phrase is now restated in measure 14, except that it is now in the second violin, while the first violin repeats what was in the second violin part. The same pattern goes from measures 15 through 16, with the harmony getting more and more outré. With the final *decrescendo* in measure 16, we come back to the original opening statement which is now played in the viola for one bar, the melody being completed by the first violin in the next three bars.

In measure 20 we have an unexpected entrance of the viola marked *espressivo* which should definitely be red-lined. It is another symptom of Ravel's building up the harmonic kingdom that is uniquely his. At measure 21 the first violin is still carrying the primary action, but the thing to be anticipated is the answer by the second violin which is marked by an accent; and this, of course, should be done with a solo *vibrato*. The total effect in measure 21 is of four quarter-notes — quarter-note number one: first violin; number two: second violin; number three: viola; and number four: back to first violin, with the ending of the phrase set off by a pizzicato "plunk" (vibrated!) from the cello. This is repeated, but with the cello *pizzicato* on the third rather than the first beat.

We are now into figure 1 with an entirely new melody played by the first violin for four measures. To get the impressionistic tonal effect Ravel is seeking, the second violin and viola need to play their parts in a way never before demanded in the quartet medium. For instance, the second violin has a series of groups of sixteenth-notes which can be played in a number of ways: he could play it *pianissimo* at the bridge, which would give him one variety of tone; he could play it *pianissimo* way over the fingerboard – another kind of tone; he could use tiny bows; or he could sweep with full bows every four notes. What I'm trying to illustrate is that the precise way of playing this particular passage is not limited, or delineated, or defined. What the musician is looking for is effect. And the effect we are looking for is the too-familiar phrase, "out of this world."

The same type of reasoning goes for the viola part, with his repeated sixteenth-notes. Because it is the second violin and viola who give the strange, otherworldly tonal impression at figure 1, their four measures are also red-lined. It is through the experience of balancing the ensemble that they will learn just how much volume to produce, how much tone to emphasize to merge with the totality of what is happening. Finally, at figure 1 the first violin will also use a new kind of tone. He may play it with a lot of *vibrato*, very soft, a lot of bow, and near the bridge. We are no longer playing Beethoven, Brahms, or Mozart. We want a new type of tone. We will definitely get it, too, which is why Ravel was deliberately chosen. He is THE composer who has produced the quintessential example of tonal impressionism for string quartet. At figure 1, even the cellist is executing a figure that is certainly not mundane. He's jumping octaves as if it were a solo concerto. Although playing softly, background and *obbligato*, he should be trying for a special type of tone and a beautiful *vibrato* so that all four voices blend in an entirely new concept of tonal imagery.

At the fifth measure after figure 1, for one and a half measures the viola takes over the lead and repeats the prime melody the first violin initiated at figure 1. Still keeping in mind that we are trying to bring out tonal impressions, when the viola performs his measure and a half prime solo, it should be played stressing viola quality to its limit – even though it's *piano* (we haven't forgotten that). In this case we would have to ask ourselves, "What is the special quality of tone we want from the viola?" Since we

114

are repeatedly discussing the tone colors that Ravel is evoking in his various manipulations of the quartet parts, what comes immediately to mind is that he should play with an amber tone—a glowing, golden tone. But while he is playing this repetition of the prime melody, the other three parts are not sitting still: we have sixteenth-notes in the first and second violins. Here now is one of those places where the cello, in playing the long notes, can make a considerable difference in the tone quality of the entire quartet by projecting lots of expression, using a plenitude of throbbing *vibrato*, a beautiful solo tone, yet still maintaining *pianissimo*.

The viola ends this luminous passage abruptly on the third beat of measure 6 where it is immediately taken over in an almost exact imitation by the second violin, running through measure 7, and the other parts repeat the same kind of ornamentation they had done in the previous measure.

Measure 8 is one of those incredible musical expressions that, on occasion, all great composers produce. Now is produced a tonal surge, with marvelous chords, of the entire quartet. The only possible lead is the fact that the second violin is playing a reminder of the original deceptively bucolic air. But the real, the important, the magical, the provocative impression of this measure is the throbbing swell done by all the instruments—like an accordion opening and closing—but in breathtaking modern harmonies, fading out, fading down into one of those rising patterns with the first violin playing sixteenth-note grouplets and the viola playing sixteenth-notes in pairs in what is essentially the arpeggiation of a fully diminished seventh chord. The same pattern is repeated at a higher pitch-level in the next two measures.

We finally come to figure 2: the first violin takes over with the original opening melody which builds up and accelerates to a tremendous climax, with the *Allegro* and the exchange of descending sixteenth-note groups by the first and second violins which continues up to the seventh bar

115

after figure 2. Here the pattern of running sixteenths is carried forward by the second violin and viola while the accordion-swells are generated by the first violin and the cello, which finally ritards into "tempo one" at one measure before figure 3.

In this bar the cello has a definite solo figure played with a concerto approach, carrying this entire attitude forward to the second measure after figure 3. In the second measure after figure 3, the cello has a rising figure which crescendos to a *mezzo piano* where the initial theme is repeated by the first violin and the other participants, in typical Ravelian harmony. In the third measure, as they end, the cello now continues his solo with a *decrescendo* coming back down to *piano*. At this time, the first violin again repeats the initial theme and the entire quartet joins in with characteristically modern harmonies.

As the first violin ends in the sixth measure after figure 3, the emphasis shifts to the second violin who is constrained to play a most beautiful solo on one note—A. At the fourth beat, the viola and cello join him for a *sforzando*, producing a most telling effect. Then, after their *decrescendo*, the first violin plays two rhythmic *pizzicato* notes, while the second violin repeats his solo of the previous measure and, again, is joined at the *sforzando* on the fourth beat by the viola and cello. It is to be noted that all during the five measures in which the same type of figuration is repeated, the last beat of the measure is represented by a *sforzando* which, in this case, will of course be a *vibrato sforzando*. (Since the whole thing is in the *piano* range of volume, a *marcato* type of *sforzando* is definitely not called for.)

This entire series of phrases alternates between the second violin's playing that single A with the loveliest possible *vibrato* tone, and by the piquant *pizzicati* of the first violin. These measures are again of a type that, until this composition, had never been heard before. The longer the quartet goes on, the more unique and individualistic it becomes.

116

Although the IDEA of the Ravel quartet has been carried forward by later composers, he is not a Beethoven or a Wagner initiating an entirely new type of music. He is one of a kind. No one can copy him.

Now the repetition of all these phrases rises to its peak at figure 4, after which the second violin decrescendos and ritards slightly through the first bar of figure 4. At this point, the viola and the first violin present an eerie melody two octaves apart conjuring up an absolutely unique effect in quartet playing. Nothing like it had ever been heard before. Their tones should blend so perfectly that it sounds like an entirely new instrument— one might say a viola with violinistic overtones, or a violin with violistic undertones. In any case, the effect is extraordinary and stands alone as one of the most beautiful passages in all music. This dual solo continues from the second bar through the ninth bar of figure 4. While this haunting melody is being played by the first violin and viola, the cello has pairs of *piano pizzicato* notes which add just the spice of flavoring that balances the whole theme and is a most important component of the eight bars. The cello should play his two *pizzicato* notes, every other bar, *piano*, but with the utmost delicacy and feeling.

At the eighth bar after figure 4, the second violin has some extremely difficult but most important sixteenth-note *arpeggi* which should not be lost while the first violin and viola are playing their luminous duo and the cello is emoting on his pizzicato quarter-notes.

The entire quartet fades away with the second violin carrying the theme for the six bars before figure 5. Here, again, the fourth and third measures before figure 5 should not be neglected by the viola who has a double *piano espressivo* counter solo to bring out, which should be performed softly but with emotion. Being a counter melody, it sets off in a most effective way the second violin and all the other things that are going on.

At figure 5, another melody starts in the first violin for five measures; then he returns to the original theme and we are now back to a repetition of our opening pages. Although there may be differences in harmony or entrances of various voices, the same exchanges of melody and stressing of notes is done from there until figure 6.

A look at the score at this point will show that red-lining the types of phrases that should be stressed by the various players has become almost automatic. The movement is getting clearer and clearer, which is the purpose for which all this comprehensive survey is being done in such detail. The same type of effect continues until the seventh measure before figure 7, on the fourth beat of which the viola enters with a new melody. As the viola terminates this unusual melody one bar before figure 7, we again have the rising grouplets of sixteenth-notes in the first and second violins in a *crescendo* to a *piano* at figure 7. Starting with figure 7, while the second violin and viola are playing a combination of running and paired sixteenth-notes, it is now the first violin and cello who repeat the melody two octaves apart and again achieve a grouping of tones with an entirely new and different sound. Here is a typical passage where we have the melody being played in a very unusual manner: two octaves apart with a completely original tone coloring which, as has been explained before, may be done in all sorts of ways. One that is highly recommended is to play extremely softly but with a lot of bow near the bridge. This will give a totally different type of tone and will create the desired effect. At the same time, the second violin and viola, although at a triple *piano* volume, should be playing their parts with all due attention to dissonant intervals, unusual types of tone, and little risings and fallins, in order to make their parts as interesting and vital as possible. The effect of strangeness will be even more enhanced if these repeated sixteenth-notes are played near the bridge, *sul ponticello*. Due attention should be paid to measures 6 and 5 before figure 8 where we have one of those accordion-like *crescendi* where the entire quartet expands and contracts. Once again, this type of tone-painting brings to our attention the fact that this quartet is tonally unique. Although written in a masterly fashion and of great interest to the listener, it is enhanced many times over by the fact that the tonal effect is so similar to that which an impressionistic picture has on the observer. The theme itself, or its development, is not the most vital thing in the quartet (or the painting), but it is the sounds (impressions) emanating from the quartet which provide the greatest impact.

At figure 8 a familiar type of melody reappears in the viola and the only thing fresh and new is the sudden injection at measure 5 of broken *arpeggi* played by the cello and the first violin. It is not to be expected that these should be played as if every note were to be heard. They are actually more like broken chords. Just as long as that unusual modern chord abruptly pierces the air, the effect is made, because, immediately, on the fourth quarter the first violin and cello enter once again into that striking melody (this time only one octave apart) which has been done before, with all the various effects repeated, but with the extra spice of these broken *arpeggi* which again appear in measure 8. The movement continues with the melody going to the viola, then to the second violin, and to the first violin who carries it upwards to a full double *forte* which, by the third measure after figure 9, becomes a triple *forte* with cello and second violin playing repeated broken chords, the melody being reinforced at the triple *forte* level by the viola.

The quartet has now reached a climax which quickly diminuendos to the *poco ritardando* where, in the third measure of the *poco meno vivo*, the second violin now has a fully outlined solo part which is reinforced by these chord *arpeggi* inserted in every other measure by the first violin. The dialogue between the first violin and the second violin and the juxtaposition of the second violin melody with the pizzicato chords of the first violin continue until the lead is taken over by the first violin through the *ritardando* and, once again, we are back to the opening in the original tempo. The quartet continues in this first movement using all the effects that we have discussed in detail up to this point; it ends with a coda which grows more and more crystal clear in its harmonies, culminating in what might be termed a smooth angelic termination which concludes this translucent movement. We might mention that, in the last five measures, attention should be paid to the fact that the second violin is playing in octave double-stops a counter solo to the first violin, and that, in the last two measures, there is a pizzicato figure carried forward by the cello and the viola, the movement ending with placid, triple *piano pizzicato* quarter-notes (viola and cello) and a heavenly chord held by the first and second violins.

SECOND MOVEMENT

The greatest difficulty in playing the second movement lies in the unusual rhythms which always seem to come on the off-beats. The initial motif starts off immediately by being marked in 6/8 and 3/4. This results, because of the accents, in the second violin's and viola's playing half the time in 2 and half the time in 3 while the theme, as projected by the first violin and aided by the cello when the cello enters uninterrupted, is in 3. This gives a type of jiggling effect so that the rhythm never quite settles down into a clear pattern, although, when played correctly, the timing in this movement is as inflexible as steel—it has to be, for the player to hang on and not get lost in these off-accents.

There really is, at least for the first seven bars, no actual stressing of any particular pattern or theme, except that the first violin is playing the melody. The one thing stressed in these first seven bars is that, while the first violin and cello are playing their parts in three beats to the bar, the second violin and viola, by virtue of their accents being played in different parts of the bar, play one measure in two, the next measure in three, and so on. Now this may sound difficult, but, the fact is, it is NOT.

There arises a problem which we will discuss at a later time, and that is, at one bar before figure 15, the second violin, viola, and cello come in after a rest and the big problem here is how to sound like one instrument or, to put it in larger perspective, how to play together in a quartet. This will be discussed in fuller detail in one of the final sections.

At figure 15, we have again entered the magic realm of Ravel's world where unusual effects, no matter how achieved, are called for. Here is a blend of running sixteenth-notes and all kinds of augmented intervals in the second violin and viola against a weirdly enchanting melody played by the first violin. Rhythmically, this section is not that difficult because the basic *pizzicato* rhythm of the cello fits in precisely with the second violin and viola, but now, again, a new element appears. The last beat of the first violin's melody in the third bar after figure 15 is 3 against 4, which is most difficult to play smoothly — certainly so in a sight-reading situation. The same pattern is now repeated with the viola as soloist in measure 5 after figure 15.

At figure 16 the viola initiates a melodic pattern — one cannot really call it a melody — which carries through to figure 18 and repeats the rhythmic motif of this entire movement, in the form of two beats to the bar played by the cello against a melody of three beats to the bar played by the viola.

This pattern is interrupted at the sixth bar after figure 16 when a motif of 3 against 2 alternating between first and second violin rises to double *forte* and decrescendos to double *piano* at figure 17. At figure 17 the rhythm becomes a comparatively simple two against three where we have three beats in the tremolo of the first violin, second violin, and viola against the two beats of the cello. In the same fashion it continues with this two against three in the various measures throughout most of the movement.

As a learning suggestion, I would say that first it should be played at a quite slow tempo with great stress on the accents and the rhythms and then, with the tempo gradually increased (by a metronome or just naturally), the pattern will fall into place by itself.

Figure 17 continues in a straightforward manner with a tremolo by the first violin and viola in a descending figure which is finally joined by the cello in the third measure after figure 17, where he plays a running eighth-note figure in *pizzicato*. The expression markings are also fairly uncomplicated, and this part is actually among the simplest and clearest parts of the whole quartet.

We now return to figure 18, which is a repetition of the movement's opening, so that the same type of analysis can be applied from figure 18 onward to figure 19; this whole section, again, is fairly obvious.

Figure 19 repeats the first part of the movement, referring back to figure 15, and goes on in a like manner to figure 21.

At figure 21 we have the familiar Ravelian *tremolo* (by the first and second violin) against rising *pizzicati arpeggi* (traded off by the viola and cello). The *crescendi* and *diminuendi* are all straightforward, and this continues in a simple, lucid manner to figure 22 which finishes up with the solo *pizzicati* by the cello who fades away to a triple *piano*, and we finally reach the first complex part of the movement: figure 22.

Care should be taken that the last six bars before figure 22 are played with solo intensity by the cello, even though very softly. The viola is bringing us another tone color (with his accented, *mezzo forte*, decrescendoing last bar where he lands on two A's). The following lines are most interesting because there are three melodies all going on at the same time. The second violin and viola play this moving chromatic type of melody with rhythmic changes and variations against a cello solo which is very smooth, melodic, and unchromatic. So here is a typical example of these complex rhythms where we have two against three, and there are frequent meter changes and all the other modern devices which Ravel uses in profusion, making the quartet one which I believe hardly any group in the world can sightread.

Usually at figure 22 the quartet starts to get shaky and, in essence, the rhythm seems to become so complex that disaster soon sets in and everybody starts yelling that they don't know where they are and they don't know what's going on and they don't understand it (Gott uns hilfe!), etc. Actually, when one examines the score, it's not that difficult: the second violin and viola play a beautiful duet in parallel major thirds, with exactly the same rhythms note for note, through five measures. As a counterpoint, the cello plays an utterly simple melody marked *très expressif*, thus indicating he should stress his part a little more in the soloistic manner than would the second violin and viola who are playing more in the nature of a counter solo.

Two unusual features about these four measures are: in every other measure there is at least a clear first beat, whereas, in the fourth measure, the cello plays two eighth-notes against a held-over triplet by the viola and second violin. This can upset—rhythmically—the other instruments, but certainly it doesn't take the greatest sophistication to play a theme built to such proportions.

Measure 5 is more complex, with a triplet in the cello against held-over eighth-notes in the second violin and viola.

In measure 6, as the viola and cello end their melodies, the first and second violins continue with their theme, and the eighth-notes almost all match. The only complexity here is that the first violin ends measure 6 with a triplet (which is tied-over from the second beat) against the final eighths of the viola and second violin. This could also cause some insecurity, but just being sure of your rhythm will certainly clarify this whole measure and, at the same time, serve as a base, because, as the viola enters, his part now becomes a handsome solo, so that everyone follows his solo for the next four measures.

Again, here is the same pattern as was defined at figure 22: the first and second violins are playing a duet in parallel eighth notes; while the viola plays the third beat of the measure with two eighth-notes, the first and second play a triplet — two against three. Still there is no great complexity, and a glance at the score should be sufficient to clear up the whole passage. There is nothing too out of the ordinary. Of course, this being Ravel, the first and second violin are playing intervals which, against the pedal note of the cello and the soaring, individualistic solo melody of the viola, create that modern atmosphere which we refer to as tone-painting — another type of impressionistic playing.

Now, at the 6/8 double bar before measure 11 after figure 22, we do have more of a problem part to play, but rhythmically it still is not that difficult. While the first violin is obviously playing the primary melody, the second violin and viola are playing the off-beats of the 6/8 rhythm — in this case it would be beats two and three, and five and six in tremolo eighth-notes — , while at the same time the cello is playing a part which balances with the first violin so that the four parts are unified. But, if the second violin and viola keep in mind that they are simply resting on one, playing two and three, resting on four, playing five and six, again, the rhythmic problems in these five measures before figure 23 are minimized.

For a moment, let us go back to figure 22 which is marked *Lent* (slow) and then *cédez* (*ritardando*) into *a Tempo*. This section does cause insecurity, and the only remedy that can be offered here is that these few bars must be repeated until what is going on is clear to all the players. In a part such as this, a score is most helpful.

At figure 23 the first violin is playing his solo against the pedal note of the cello, and the second violin and viola are playing *legato* off-beats. This can give a feeling of uncertainty, but a glance at the score will show that this, too, is quite straightforward. The phrase finally ends with second violin and viola paired in a *decrescendo*, and we return to the pervasive viola solo for another two measures.

Throughout the last measures we've had the high viola solo and the ensemble should keep in mind that Ravel's primary objective in writing this quartet was not simply melodies, rhythms, and harmonies of the 20th century—although these are all extremely important—but that here music is meeting Monet, Manet, Van Gogh, and all the rest of the Impressionists on their own ground, for the first time, in a musical masterwork. The combination of all the diverse elements in harmony, rhythm, and types of tone used by the various players is of a unique type to which we can only, again, apply the words "impressionistic tone color." This is the peak of tone-painting in music—where the elements of sensuous harmonies and unusual tonal qualities of the various instrumental combinations are stressed above all else. This aspect of the Ravel quartet is what makes the greatest impact. It also serves as the model and forerunner for all the quartets yet to be written.

From figure 23 on, the viola solo continues and ends on the sixth bar after figure 23 when, after some interesting *pizzicati* and running eighth-notes in paired second violin and cello, there is a *rallentando* leading into the solo part of the first violin accompanied by figuration in the second violin and viola.

In the second bar of this *a Tempo*, we again have an example of this quartet's unique qualities. I would like to emphasize that Ravel is the one who really established a one-of-a-kind example which serves as a goal for modern quartet playing and composition. As you go through the score you find that at certain intervals there is a very clear leading solo and melody, but most of the time all four parts are approximately equal.

The conclusion that I want to apply to the whole quartet is that, finally, the quartet form has evolved to the point where it is an ensemble of four soloists. Most of the time all the parts are equally important.

This particular measure, which is one bar before the 3/4 *a Tempo*, is a perfect example. There is no doubt the first violin is terminating his solo lead. At the same time, there is an extremely interesting rising and falling in thirty-second-notes by the paired second violin and viola. Simultaneously the cello is holding a note which jumps up an octave and back down again, and can be played very beautifully, almost with solo quality, to match everything else that's going on. It continues with a first violin solo which is actually a repetition of what went before. The same type of expressive playing would be applied here.

One bar before figure 24 is perfectly straightforward, except that the second violin and viola have technically quite difficult parts to play, especially since they are being pushed by the *pressez* indication in the music.

Now we reach figure 24 and, as the first and second violin are playing a *legato tremolo*, the cello and then the viola in *pizzicato* partially recall the opening theme. In the next measure the viola plays a fragment of a theme we have already heard and then, as he goes into fast *arpeggi*, this opening *pizzicato* theme played first in the cello recurs and then is played by the first and second violins.

In measure 4 after figure 24, the cellist has to be careful that his *pizzicati* match the rhythm of the second violin; a mismatch would lead to everybody's getting lost. In that sense, here is a pitfall, and again I must mention that a score would be most helpful. In essence, the rhythm is still comparatively simple. All through this movement we are showing through this detailed analysis of the score that, although rhythmically it may sound quite complicated, actually it is simple and more "square" than we might expect.

126

In this same manner, at figure 25 a primary theme is played by the first violin with the second violin playing broken *pizzicato* chords which lend an unusual background to the melody, and broken *arpeggi* played in triplet sixteenths by the viola. Straightforward counting is a must here. All through this passage, which ends at the 3/4 double bar, the cello is holding a pedal tone which serves as the foundation for all the harmonies in the upper voices and should not be neglected but played with a lovely *vibrato*; it is definitely a pedal tone and not a featured note such as often occurs in other pedal tones of this type.

As we arrive at five bars before figure 26, we are repeating what we have done previously. There are no new problems. The same analysis and performance should be applied to the remaining measures until we reach figure 26.

As figure 26 ends the phrase *pianissimo* with a chord held by the first violin and viola, the cello starts a running figure in eighth-notes as a *pizzicato* solo for four bars, whereupon the viola takes it up, and at the sixth bar after figure 26 the first violin plays a *reprise* of the movement's opening. A perusal of the score shows that everything matches exactly. It is in 6/8; the viola is playing six eighth-notes per bar; the others are playing either quarter-notes or eighth-notes exactly within the duple rhythm of the bar. There is no reason to become insecure at this point. It is crystal clear. It is simply a matter of nobody's jumping ahead or behind but keeping the rhythm going with exactitude.

Once the music is familiar, there can be certain latitudes taken with it, as, for instance, the ninth bar after figure 26. The second violin has accents on the first and fourth eighth-notes of each measure. The rest of the quartet comes in on beat number five so it sounds like an off-beat—one, two, three, four, FIVE, six—there is nothing misleading about the whole thing. Also, at this very measure, the second violin takes over the *pizzicato* solo and leads the way for nine bars, at which point there is sort of a playful off-beat movement with the second violin on the beat and the first violin off the beat (yum, PUM, pum, PUM), which continues for four bars until figure 27 is reached.

At figure 27 we have scaled the heights of the movement. The initial theme is repeated in full, grand chords— pizzicato—played by first and second violin as the viola and cello drum the six eighth-notes of each bar. And so it goes on, absolutely straightforwardly. There is one measure, the sixth bar after figure 27, in which the first violin is playing in 3/4, but the accent of the 6/8 bar eighth-notes, played by the second violin and viola, are on the first, third and fifth eighth-notes so that it matches up perfectly. This continues on until the dramatic entrance of the first violin two and two-thirds bars before figure 28, where the rhythm of the first violin matches the second violin's *pizzicato* notes which are being played in 3/4. This is the only rhythmically tricky part of the whole movement. The opening measure of the movement is marked 6/8 and 3/4 at the same time. In this case, the second violin is playing in 3/4 and the first violin synchronizes with him, which makes it comparatively simple for those two instruments, while the viola and cello continue to play their six eighth-notes per measure. Since the pulse of their measure is in two, there is a possibility of being rhythmically upset. The strongest suggestion I can make here is to hang on to the rhythm you know is there. You also know from going through the score that there are no surprises in this movement and that if you play it exactly as written, it's going to come out correctly. You have that assurance.

From figure 28 to the end of the movement it is a repetition of the styles that have gone before and a detailed analysis does not seem required, so we now go to the third movement.

THIRD MOVEMENT

The difficulties of this movement are the changes in tempo and rhythm which occur very frequently, so the tendency to become insecure is multiplied. Usually, even with players of the highest caliber, on a sightreading basis this is the movement where things break down. However, as usual, looking through the score is the single greatest help in playing a piece of new music and, strange to say, it's rarely done.

It starts out with a graceful viola solo: very simple, a long held note, one eighth-note down, back to the held note, a triplet, and ending up with a vibrated half-note. The fact that the first two bars are in four and the second two bars are in three doesn't cause any problem. The difficulty is that the first violin, second violin, and cello come in out of the blue, so to speak. True, as written, you can see by looking at the score that it is actually the second beat. The viola plays "one." Now, where is "two"? Here we are entering a realm of ensemble playing which cannot be rhythmically preset. One school would say that in a situation of this kind, the natural leader (in this case, the first violin) simply gives the beat. In other words, the viola starts out, "one," and the first violin comes in with body English showing the "two." However, there is another type of organization which, clearly on a higher level of communication, makes entrances WITHOUT conducting. This type of playing has reached a metaphysical level. If there are no signals when to start, the players have to feel what's going on in each other's minds. Or maybe the signals are so subtle and so small that the audience cannot see what is going on. In any case, the usual method is, in a situation such as occurs in these first four bars, the beats are indicated by the leader of the moment—here, the first violin.

There is some rhythmic complexity here, because although all three instruments come down on the second beat, the cello plays an eighth-note, whereas the first violin does not, so that the players must be familiar with the content of the first four measures. Once this is done, which takes no more than a glance at the score, it is not difficult.

But if you just put the music in front of you and say, "Let's play," chaos sets in immediately.

In this case examining the score is required and the leadership of the first violin is of the greatest help. When we go on to the fifth bar and back to 4/4 time, the cello takes up this simple melody of a long note with an eighth-note at the end and back to the long note and then a triplet — very, very elementary. The other three instruments play the rhythmic pattern with which the quartet opened, and are to be led — in this case — by the first violin, through the same rhythmic problem of one instrument's playing an eighth while the others are not.

The cello finishes his solo with one bar in 3/4 time and ends up with a bar in common time marked *Pressez légèrement* where he is holding his long note — still the prime soloist, so that the *crescendo* should be of solo caliber with lots of *vibrato* and the top level of quartet solo playing.

After this 3/4 bar of rest, we must depend on the leader to give us our rhythm, in this case the first violin, who activates the other three players into a *tremolo* figure for two measures *Pressez* and then back to the first *a Tempo*.

The *a Tempo* is simplicity itself rhythmically, because it consists only of second violin, viola, and cello playing *tremolo* notes while the first violin now plays the original theme of the long note with one descending eighth-note, back to the long note, a triplet, and ending with a hold which resolves in the other instruments. The only thing to watch for in these four bars before figure 1 is that the first violin enters on an off-beat and has some tied eighth-notes which give the effect of being off the beat.

The easiest way to accomplish this phrase is for the first violin to give a downbeat every once in a while; probably the most practical thing would be to give the downbeat of each measure.

The four bars end with a hold which resolves in the second violin and viola. The first violin continues to hold and then, rather suddenly, there is a totally new melody carried by the viola from figure 1 to the common time *Très calme*. With typical moving legato eighth-notes in the second violin and a vibrated descending note pattern in the cello, all the voices weave in and out and finally come together at the *Très calme*, whereupon the *pianissimo* first violin recalls an impression of one of the primary melodies of the first movement.

At the same time, the other instruments are all playing the matching twentieth-century harmonies which make these two measures definitely impressionistic. These measures are also memorable for the fact that, in addition to these fresh new harmonies, we have a tonal quality required which is again in the impressionistic tone palette. With all four parts still in *pianissimo*, an extraordinary effect should be attempted. In this case, one suggestion might be that everyone play it over the fingerboard with a tremendous amount of expression, a total blending of subtly vibrated sounds, so that we get a *nouvelle* quality of tone. It is not an organ sound, although the chords and the melody could be for such an instrument. It is rather more of a far-off mistiness that we want for a totally different sound picture.

In the third measure of *Très calme*, the viola once again picks up the primary theme and carries it through until the second measure before figure 1. He is characteristically countered by the second violin and *espressivo* cello octave leaps *crescendo* so that, as the four measures end with the viola dying out to finish the phrase, the second violin plays four eighth-notes and a quarter-note which are equally important.

At two measures before figure 2, we repeat the same type of sound, enhanced if possible from what we had at the *Très calme*. It is the same theme in the first violin, only a fifth higher, and we are searching for a mysterious, unusual sound as the music approaches figure 2.

At figure 2 the second violin takes up the primary part and on the third beat is joined by the viola and then the cello, all three of which are balanced. We note, again, that in modern quartets we are realizing more and more the pinnacle of quartet playing. There is no longer a set melody with accompaniment, but all two, three, or four voices are playing independently and yet joining in wonderful harmonies and unusual rhythms to form a complete whole, so that no one part is actually more important than the other. We repeat, it is thus that the quartet becomes a group — an ensemble — of four individualists melded into one new voice which is that unique form: the String Quartet.

This type of playing continues, in various ways, until figure 3. A perusal of the score will quickly show that all four parts are equally important. Nobody takes a back seat to anybody. In this fashion, we no longer have to analyze who should be doing what, or who should be predominant, or who should stress what. Everybody's part is equally important. Every once in a while, a little bit of a solo may crop up, but within a measure or so, the motif is repeated in other parts; another instrument enters with a new melody, the cello is holding his beautiful long notes or playing a counter theme and, as I have now repeated a number of times, there are no longer any particular individual solo parts.

At three measures before figure 4 this *misterioso* fingerboard playing recurs with the first violin leading the same motif, terminating just before figure 4, with the cello *crescendoing* to a *forte* into a very *énergique* theme for one measure. As he holds his final note, the other three instruments enter *forte* with a lot of energy in repetition of the third movement's opening theme.

Thus they start the *ritardando*. While decelerating, all must still pay careful attention to the count which is now off-beat. The cello should be aware that, when the other three conclude, he finishes his melody leading into the *Tempo moderato.*

Three measures after figure 4, a new effect is introduced with the *legato tremolo* of the three upper instruments while the cello holds his pedal note for five measures. Of special interest here is the fact that the second measure of the *a Tempo moderato* is played by a combination whose third beat consists of a group of five notes by the first violin, six by the second violin, and seven notes in that same time period by the viola. Obviously, it is impossible to match five against six against seven. Again we have this impressionistic approach (which, by the way, was used by Wagner in "Siegfried Idyll" and Berlioz, who also wrote parts that were unplayable), because what is wanted here is a sweep of tone where the harmony cannot be classified, but the effect of the cascade of notes really will be unclear if any of the three players plays his third beat at full strength. This same *modus operandi* is repeated in the three measures before figure 5.

Again going back to the *a Tempo moderato*, the important thing is that we are trying for another tone color. The suggestion here is that, although double *piano* by everyone, the *legato tremoli* should be played near the bridge. We thus get a very French tone. Then, when the five against six against seven notes come on the third beat of the second measure, there would be a little stress emphasis, almost a *crescendo*, and then a quick drop, effecting a different tone color. When the violin is played in this manner—that is, double piano near the bridge—we get a reedy tone color.

At *a Tempo moderato* we are striving for a sound reminiscent of one of the double reed instruments—somewhere between an oboe and a piccolo. In any event, it is as far from the Mozartean type of sound as we can get, and it is definitely impressionistic. It is sound created more for the sake of the color than for the sake of what is actually going on, which, at this point, is not very significant.

As we approach figure 5, there is a reprise of some of the previous effects with the *forte* cello and the rest of the ensemble's entering on the next measure; then a repetition of the *legato tremolo* and the five against six against seven on the last beat. Care should be taken that, on the fourth bar before figure 6, the cello enter confidently as a soloist — definitely as a soloist — and give us a *bravura* rising *arpeggio* until he flourishes his high note which diminuendos ending *piano*, with the *piano* viola and double *piano* second violin.

At figure 6 we have another tone color. As the second violin plays a simple, pensive melody for five bars modified by the wraithlike *arpeggi* of the first violin accompanied by *pizzicati* in the cello every few notes, we have a fresh and different tone color. Somehow the harmony is moving away from us and going farther and farther off into a distance, removing itself from the quartet style that we have grown accustomed to over the past one hundred fifty years.

At three bars before figure 7, the viola enters with a very expressive theme punctuated by a rising *pizzicato* figure in the cello, which has a *crescendo* from a double *piano* to a *mezzo forte*, so that the simple melody that the second violin started at figure 6 has evolved into an unbelievably beautiful twentieth-century blending of harmonies, melodies and effects: a totally new tone color.

At figure 7, there is a repetition at a different pitch-level of the previous three measures, but scored altogether differently, and this type of arrangement is continually developed and magnified through the *modérément animé* and the common time measures, finally ending in a *rallentando* concluding at figure 8.

At figure 8, we repeat the effects that we have already been through, although double *forte passioné*; there is a *ritardando* before the double bar of the common time, and for four measures we hark back to that *misterioso Très calme* that we have already played a number of times. The same quality of tone color is called for. In fact, except for watching the rhythms, all the notes and bars that we now continue with have been done before.

We may mention that at figure 9, the viola has a solo passage that continues until the end of the seventh bar after

134

figure 9. Keeping in mind that the upbeat to the fifth measure after figure 9 is taken over by the cello (with a most effective virtuoso passage which crescendos and decrescendos and then, from a double *piano*, sweeps up for a measure, whereupon the scale is taken over by the first violin), at three measures before figure 10 we seek to create another tone color.

Led by the first violin, we are now in completely different harmonies, which can quickly be pointed out by the fact that, although the key signature is six flats, everybody has naturals and sharps. Although still in double *piano*, the tone color now is developed by the unusual harmonies; everybody is playing double *piano tremolo* a very unusual melody in the high first violin—we are searching for another color. This one would be more of a wiry sound, and a suggestion here would be that, while the second violin, viola, and cello are tremoloing double *piano* near the bridge, the first violin may also play softly near the bridge but with full bows. This will give an unusual effect. It is one of maybe half a dozen effects, but the basic idea is still there: we want a new sound. We want a new color, and Ravel has given us the material for creating it. He has given us outrageous harmonies, unorthodox leaps in the melodies.

Now that we have our new sound, we gradually bring it to a *crescendo* which climaxes at figure 10 in a *forte*. The first violin comes down while the viola rises. As the first violin ends in measure two, the viola takes over. The first and second violins play a syncopated figure at beat two and three, while the viola continues his solo. And finally we are back to the original viola solo which came early in the movement.

The solo ends at measure 7 after figure 10, and for a few measures the viola again recalls one of the first movement melodies, but, due to the contrapuntal melody of the first violin and the "different" harmonies in second violin and cello, we are again moving into a unique tonal atmosphere. The harmony and the counterpoint in these three measures are unusual enough that no special effect need be tried for, except, possibly, a lot of bow nearer the fingerboard, all in double *piano*. This terminates with a *rallentando* of the viola leading into figure 11, when we have another version of the movement's opening and the viola carries the major part of the theme.

This same type of movement continues; the cello will play a few important notes; the other instruments have a *pizzicato*; we have some more *tremoli* which go through the *Très lent* as the *rallentando* continues; the viola brings in one beautiful note terminated by a rolling *pizzicato* chord in the cello; the viola gives us a continuation of his melody, *crescendo and decrescendo*; and, as the first violin gives us the final remembrance of that opening theme, the cello plays his concerto-like rising melody for one bar at the third measure before the end, taken up by the viola, which is counterpointed by the second violin playing again that first original melody. And finally all four instruments end the movement with the same motif, finished by the cello, while the entire ensemble comes together in what can only be termed a heavenly chord.

FOURTH MOVEMENT

The fourth movement is rather straightforward. The only difficulties inherent in its performance stem from the fact that the speed of the movement is so great that it demands tremendous technical facility; the slightest hesitation will produce immediate chaos. Once more, we must repeat that there is no one single part, at any time, that really predominates in the performance. Each part is equally important. For instance, at six bars before figure 15 the second violin and viola are playing agitated double *forte* sixteenth-notes in a *decrescendo* for several bars. The first violin and cello are playing dotted half-notes with the first crescendoing and the cello and the others decrescendoing to approximately a *mezzo forte* at three bars before figure 15 where they are joined by the first violin who now also decrescendos, all ending at figure 15 where the first violin leads a new theme marked *espressivo*. At the same time the *sans ralentir* compels the first violin to "wing his way" through this melody without undue emphasis, proceeding smoothly and calmly (although, at the speed with which the movement is played, this is especially difficult).

At figure 16, we have again one of those backward glances, with the first violin this time playing a long theme taken note for note from the first movement, and slowing down a little bit into the *a Tempo* six bars before the next 5/4.

Here again, the last two measures before the 5/4 have a ritard, *espressivo*, and then occurs a jump back to the *a Tempo* in 5/4 where the cello is playing a motif in paired sixteenth-notes with accents on the first beat, on the second half of the third beat, and so on. His measure is divided into two in a fast 5/4 meter. The other three are playing with breaths . . . this is the point where everybody stops. (Nobody can go on. It's too hard! My advice is to stop playing.)

The four measures before figure 17 may look bizarre upon examination of the score, because it is impossible to figure out the actual rhythm. For instance, the cello is playing with accents on one and three-and-a-half of a 5/4 bar. However, in actuality, it turns out to be quite simple. The first violin, second, and viola are playing two-pulse measures and the cello is playing in two groups of five in each measure, so that, in effect, although the time signature calls for a 5/4 measure, in practice one can treat them as if they are really 2/2 measures gradually fading into figure 17.

From figure 17 onwards we have the same problems that have been discussed before where the beat and the rhythm are resolutely straightforward and square. When it says 3/4, there are three beats to the bar. When it says 5/8, there are two beats to the bar. There are no surprises, no complex rhythms that will cause any rhythmical problems. The difficulties in this last movement, as mentioned before, are that the speed is so fast that the changing tempos and the pace at which the notes are played actually remain the same except for a specifically marked *poco ritardando*, as at five bars before figure 25. It is simply that the players must get used to not being affected by the change in the time signature, so that when it goes from 5/4 to 5/8 to 3/4, etc., they should not let themselves be thrown by the fact and just simply keep beating away and maintaining the pace.

The suggestions I would make in this movement are, until it is completely mastered, it should be approached in two ways: 1) each part should be played with authority; there should be no tentative playing; do not let the rhythms get away from you; make sure you keep the accent and the beat going; and 2) since speed in itself is the single hardest obstacle of this movement, it should be played slowly until the rhythmic simplicity of the movement becomes crystal clear, and then keep repeating the movement until it can be brought up to full tempo. Such practice will help achieve consummate mastery of the entire movement.

The obstacle in the last movement is that, since it is played so swiftly, the changes in time-signature and the occasional *rallentandi* are almost sure to throw any player off the track and thus stop the movement. One must accept these facts and go through the "woodshedding" that the movement requires. Keep the beat steady, dynamic, accentuated, and positive. Practice starting very slowly, and gradually work up to tempo. If these two points will be carried out, the movement will gradually become rhythmically stable. It is technically difficult, but that is the way the music was written and there is little one can do except practice more and become a better player.

The same idea of starting slowly, dissecting each rhythmically difficult bar and gradually building up to a tempo also applies to the previous movement (or movements). This is the musical philosophy through which one may conquer the Ravel (or any other) quartet.

138

I might add one last note that, although I have played in many quartets—from fine professional to weak amateur—we have never yet been able to play through the Ravel without stopping. I sincerely believe it can be done by applying the suggestions noted here.

That one does not have to be grave to be serious seems to be the message of this ensemble of smiles.

SUMMARY

The basic premise of this book is that quartets have evolved, both in composition and in performance, from the idea of a leading concerto-type player doing 95% of the themes and the others serving as background accompaniment, to the modern approach (exemplified by the Guarneri Quartet) where the ensemble becomes a fusion of four virtuoso artists—each part being equally important in its own fashion. Also, the more modern quartets (of which the Ravel is a prime example) are composed with the parts being intentionally equally balanced and important.

Of prime importance is the fact that the finest modern quartet players have carried this musical philosophy back to Haydn and Mozart which are then performed with equal attention and artistry applied to each individual part. The result achieved is that such performance of the familiar classics (ranging from Haydn through Brahms) issues forth almost as a revelation of what the String Quartet is capable of producing.

NEUNZEHNTES QUARTETT
für 2 Violinen, Viola und Violoncell
von
W. A. MOZART.
Köch. Verz. No 465.

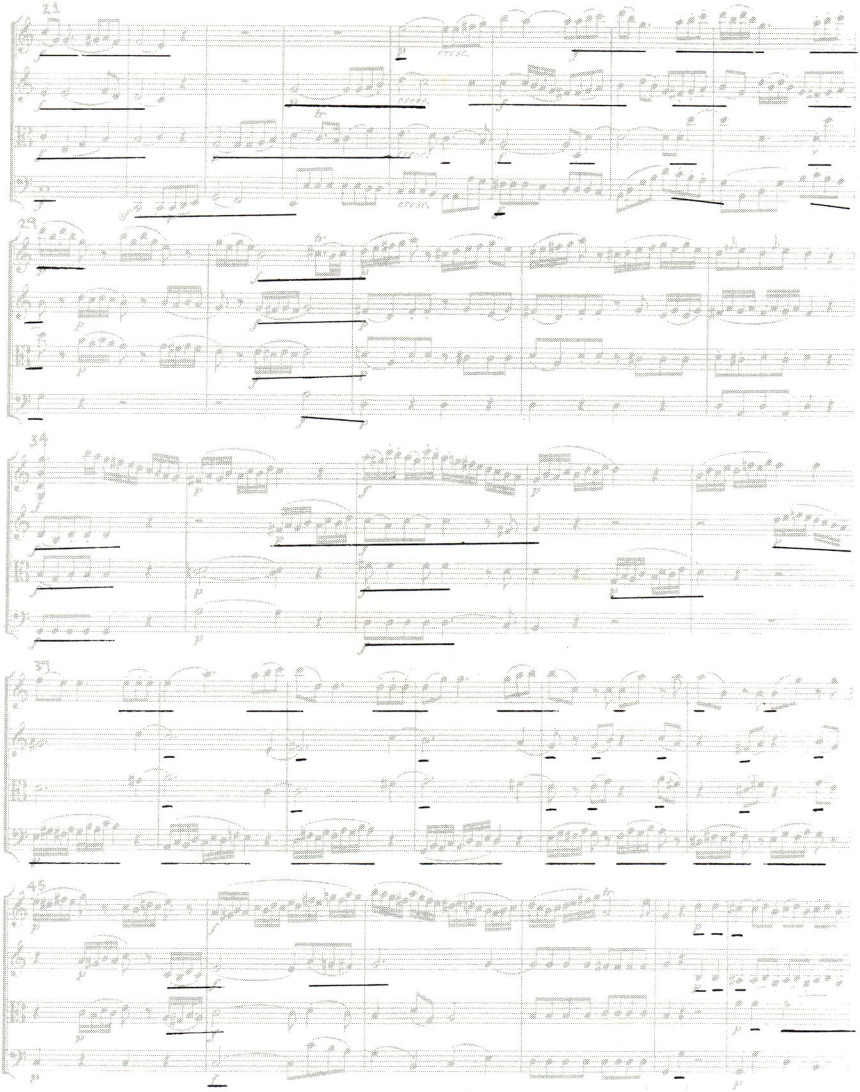

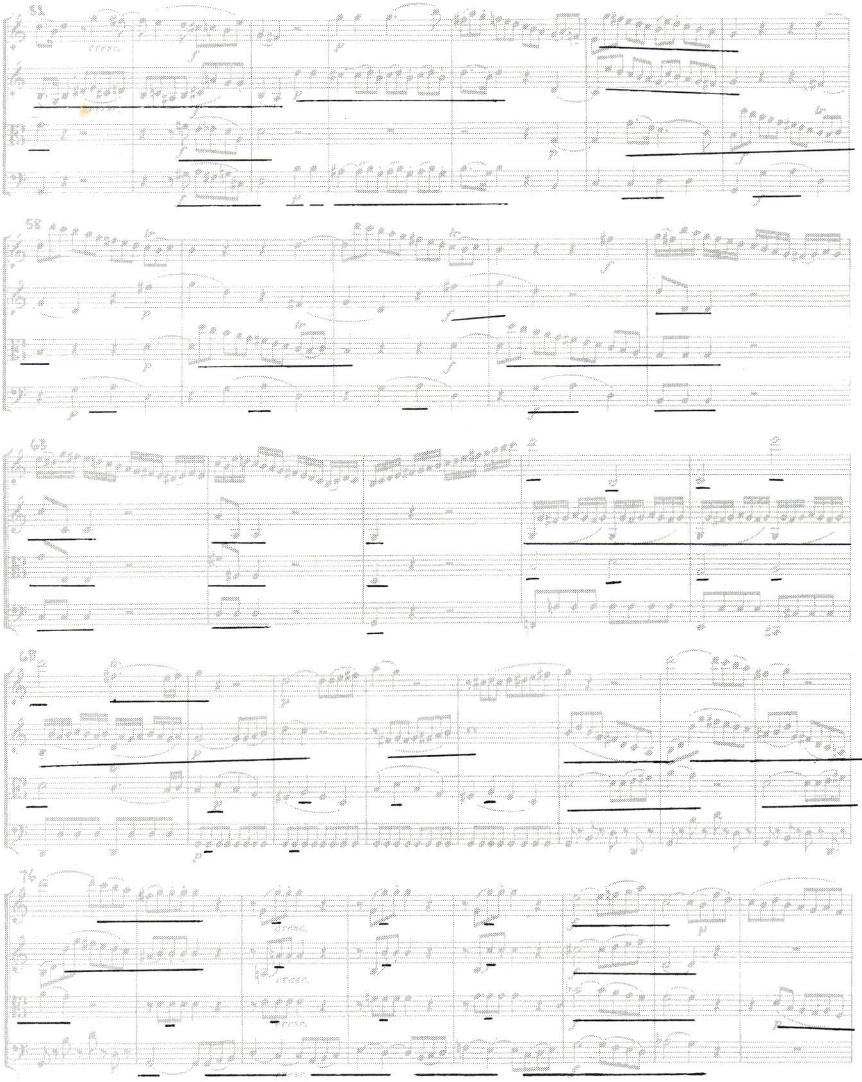
cresc.

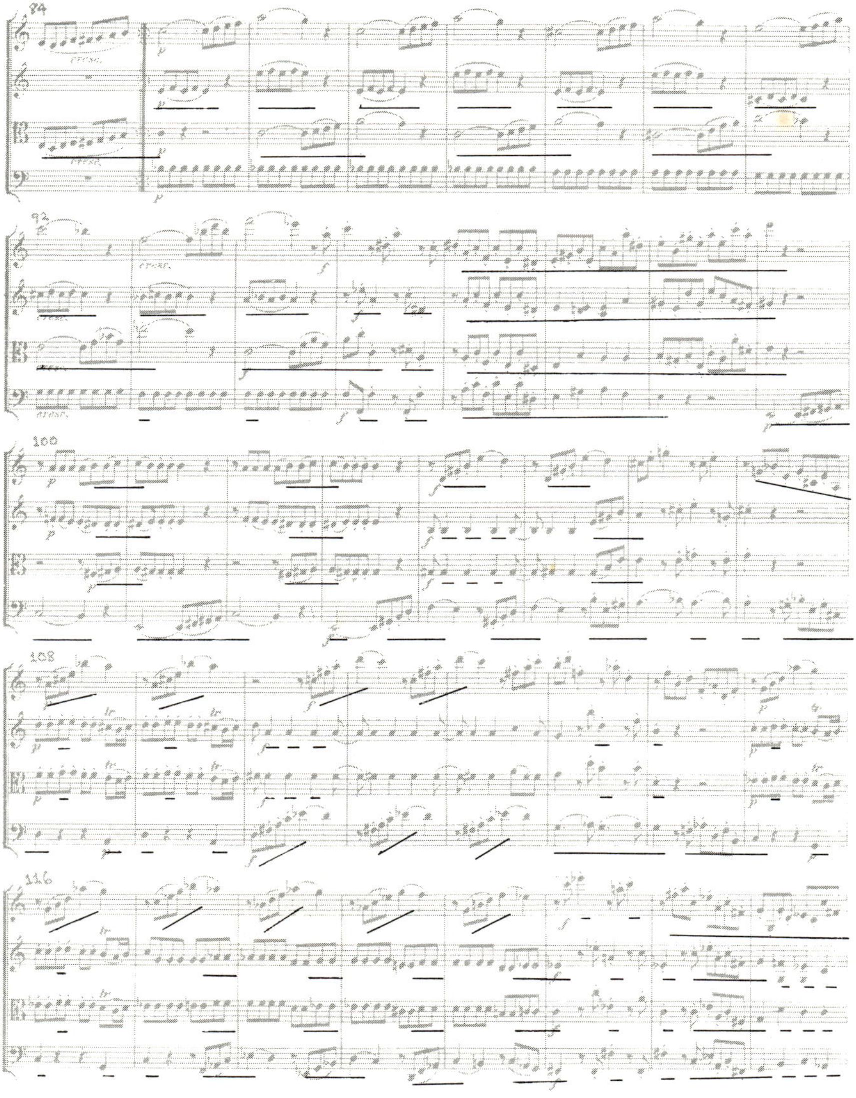
84
cresc.
92
100
108
116

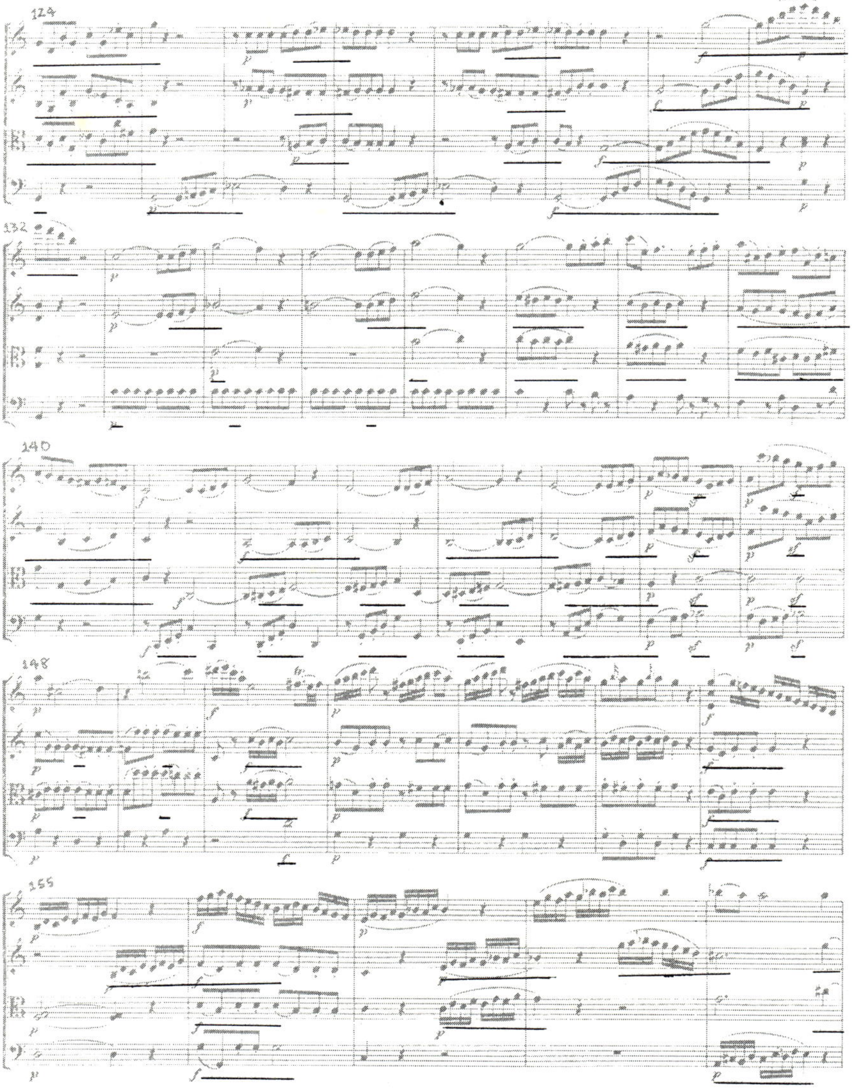
124
132
140
148
155

148

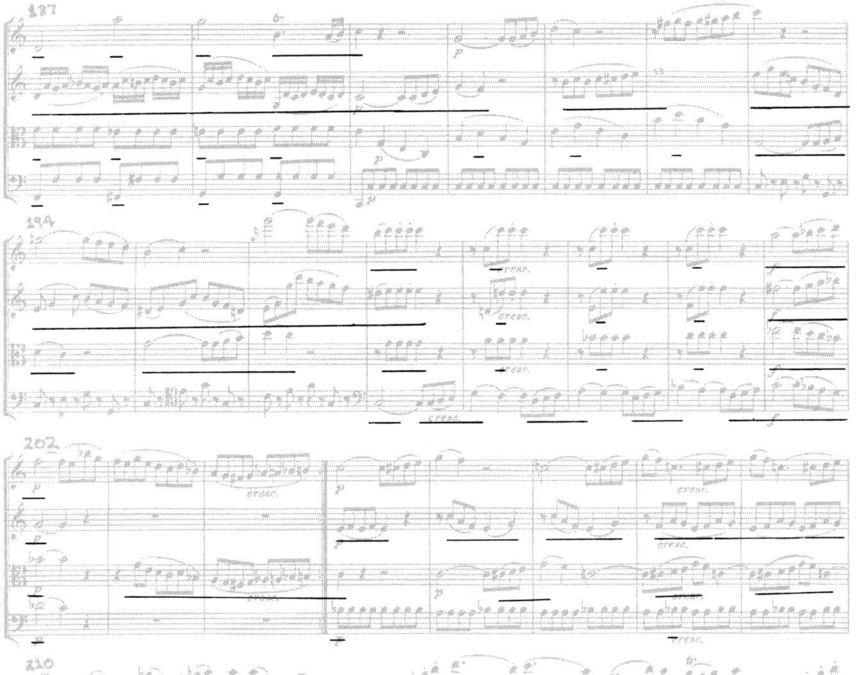
202
cresc.

DREI QUARTETTE

für 2 Violinen, Bratsche und Violoncell

von

L. van BEETHOVEN.

Dem Grafen Rasoumoffsky gewidmet.

Op. 59. Nº 2.

Quartett Nº 8.

30
sempre f
sempre f
sempre f
sempre f
36
p
p
41
cresc.
cresc.
cresc.
cresc.
p dolce
p dolce
p dolce
p dolce
46
cresc.
cresc.
cresc.
cresc.
p dolce
p dolce
p dolce
53
p
dolce
pp
pp
pp
pp
p

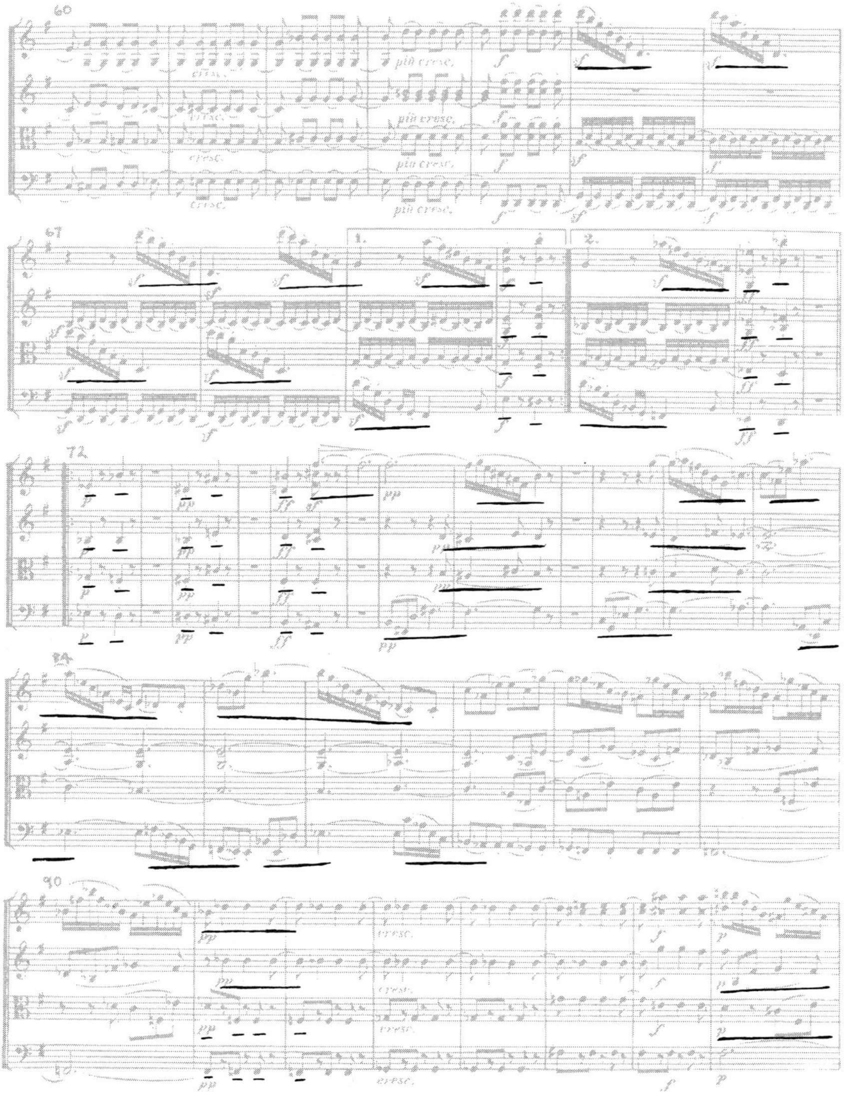
60
cresc.
più cresc.
67
1.
2.
72
90
cresc.

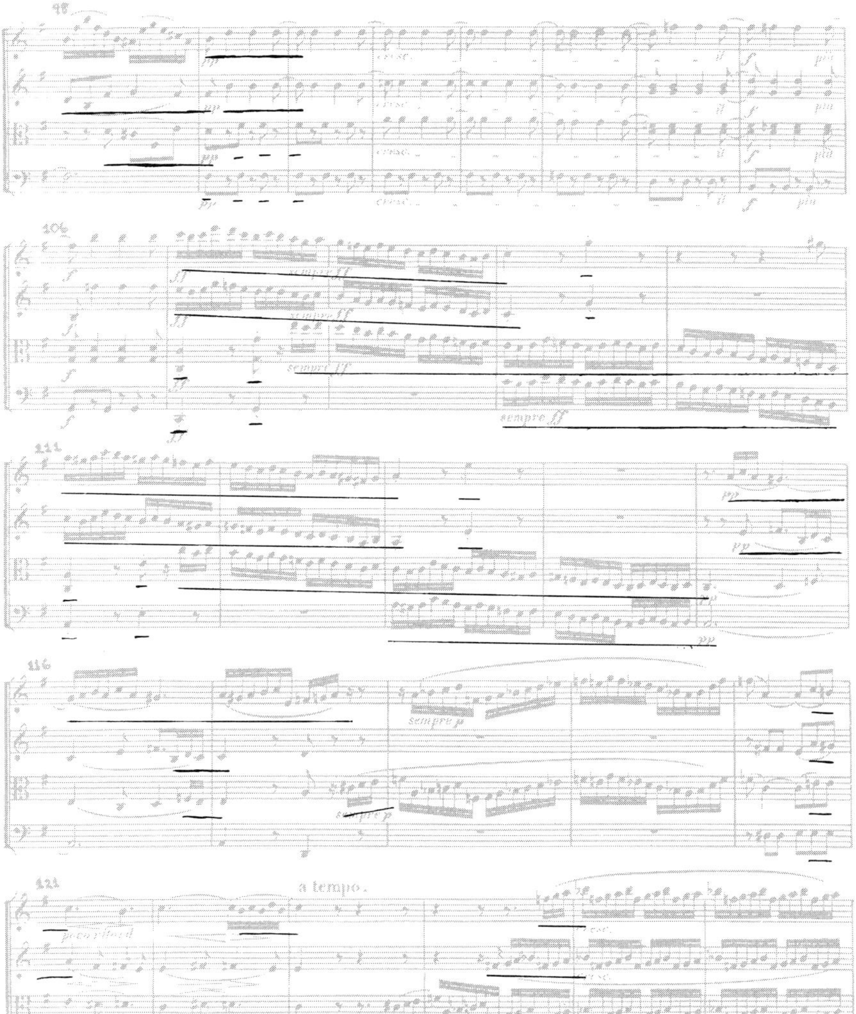
cresc.
sempre ff
sempre p
poco ritard.
a tempo.

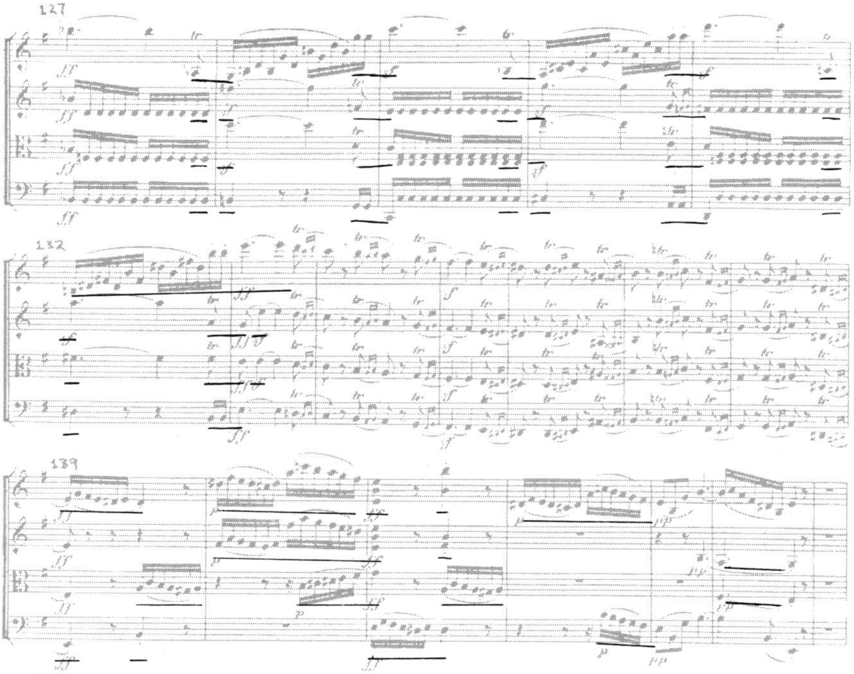
127
ff
132
139
146
pp
155
sempre p
cresc.

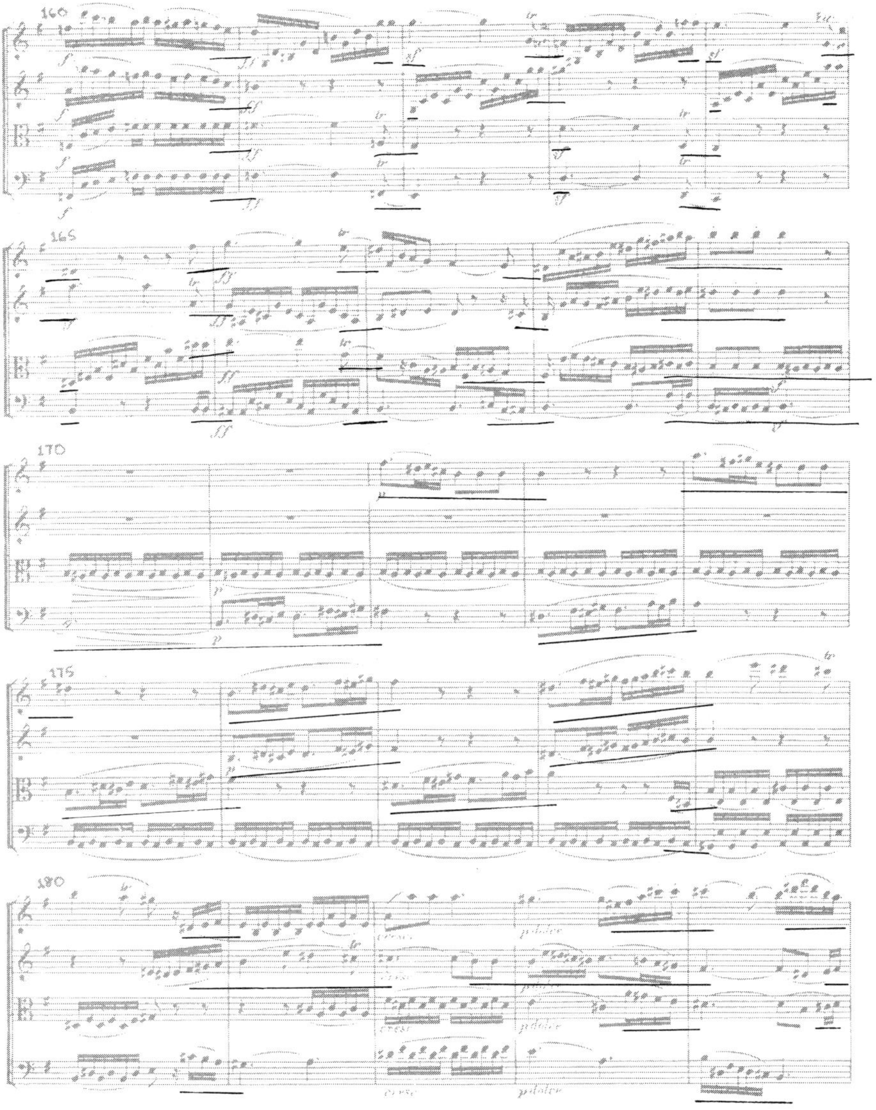
160
165
170
175
180

185
cresc.
191
p dolce
dolce
198
pp
cresc.
più cresc.
206
piano
209
pp
più p

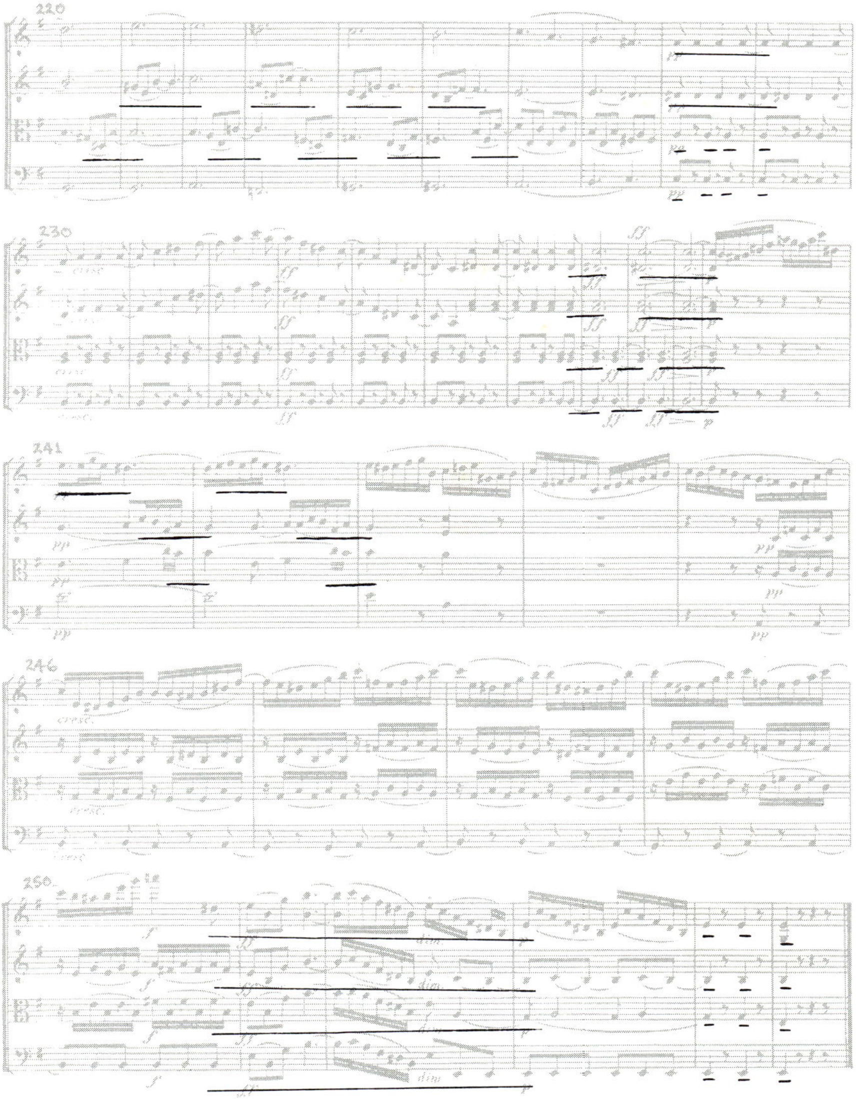
220
230
cresc.
ff
241
pp
246
cresc.
250
f
dim.

QUARTET

I

MAURICE RAVEL
(1875-1937)

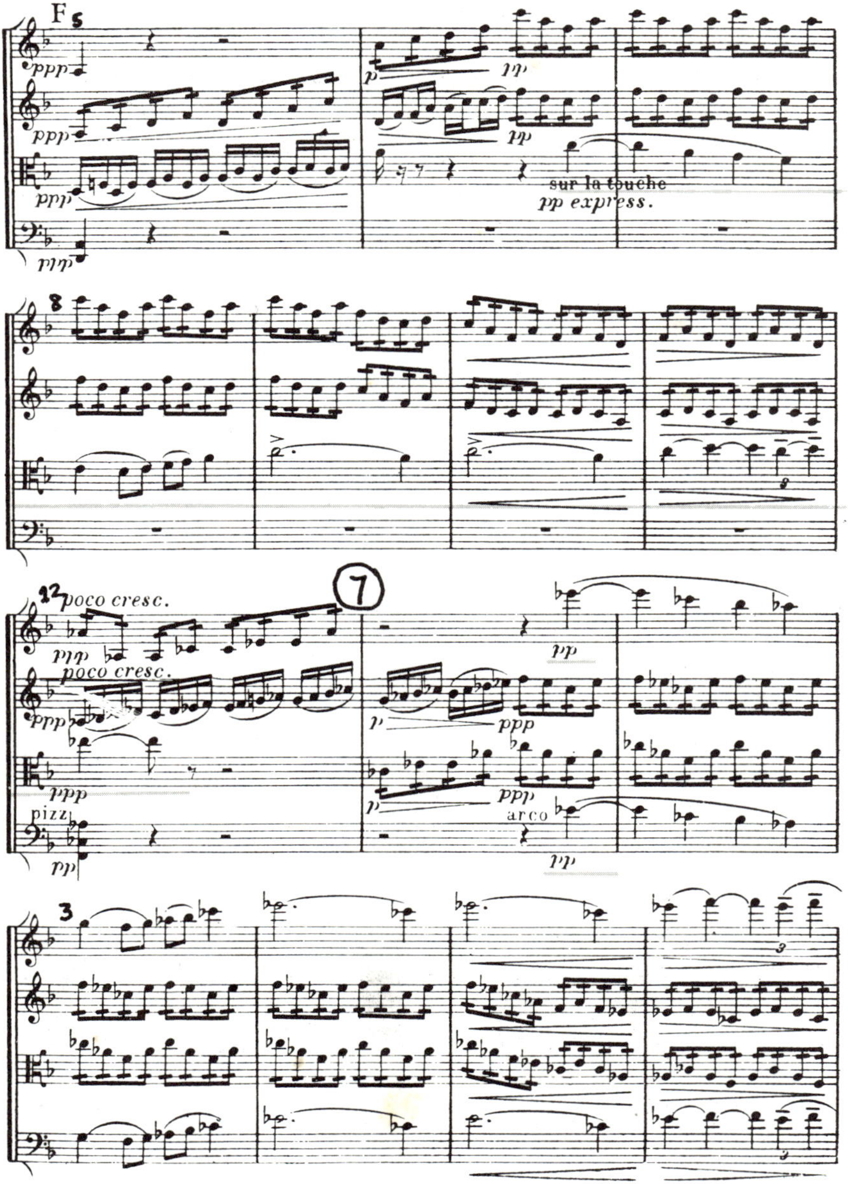
F
ppp
p
pp
sur la touche
pp express.
poco cresc.
7
pizz.
arco

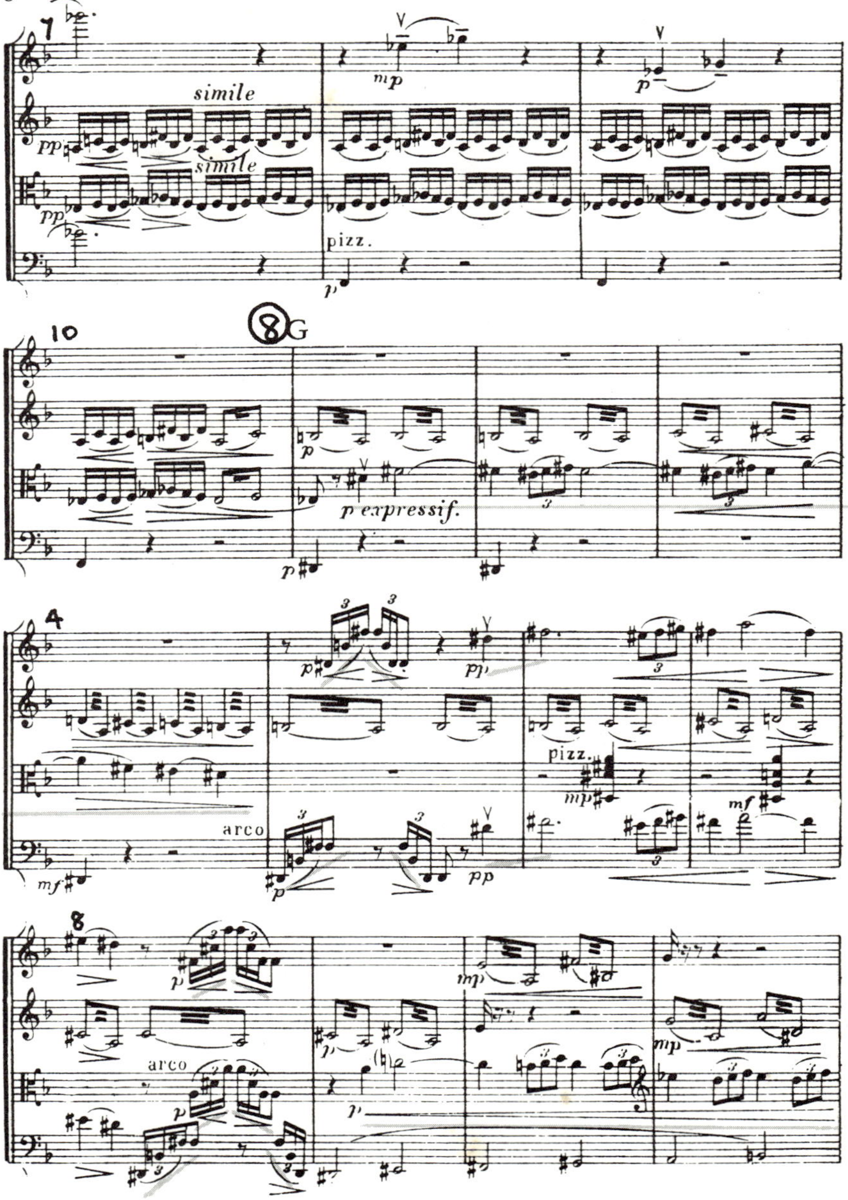
simile
simile
pizz.
p expressif.
arco
pizz.
arco

cres - cendo e accelerando poco
12
mf
p subito
9
a
poco
ff
H
Poco meno vivo
fff
4
un poco dim.
poco rit.
4e. Corde
f vibrato
p
f
7
pizz.
arco V
rit.
mf
mp

14
cédez légèrem^t.
p
arco
un peu plus lent
rall.
pp
mp
jusqu'à la fin.
mf
Lent
rall.
pp
pizz.
p
ppp

II

Assez vif _ Très rythmé ($\downarrow$. = 92)

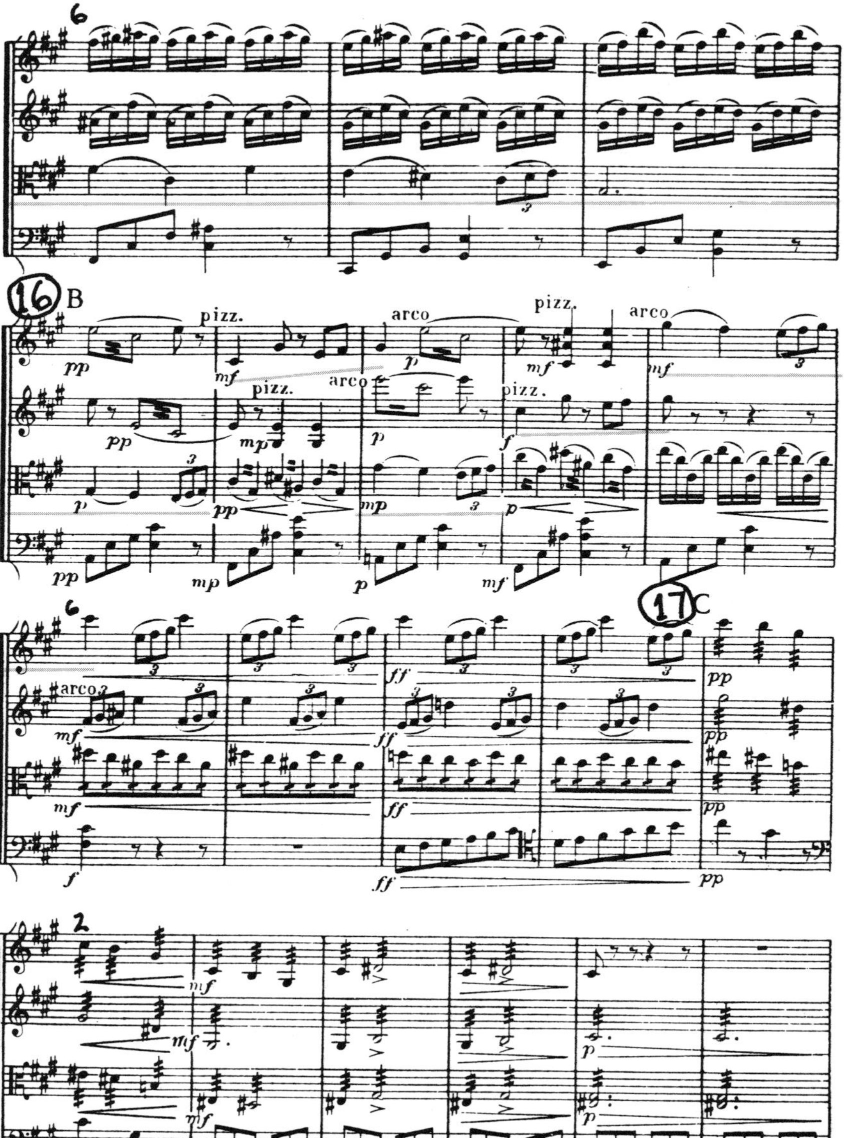
B
pizz.
arco
pizz.
arco
pizz.
arco
pizz.
arco
arco
C

18
D
pizz.
p
ppp
pizz.
p
ppp
pizz
f
pp
ff
ff
ff
ff
ff
f
mp
mp
mp
mp
mp
arco
pp
tr
f
f
ff
f
ff
f
ff
19
E
pp bien chanté
arco
ppp
arco
ppp
pp

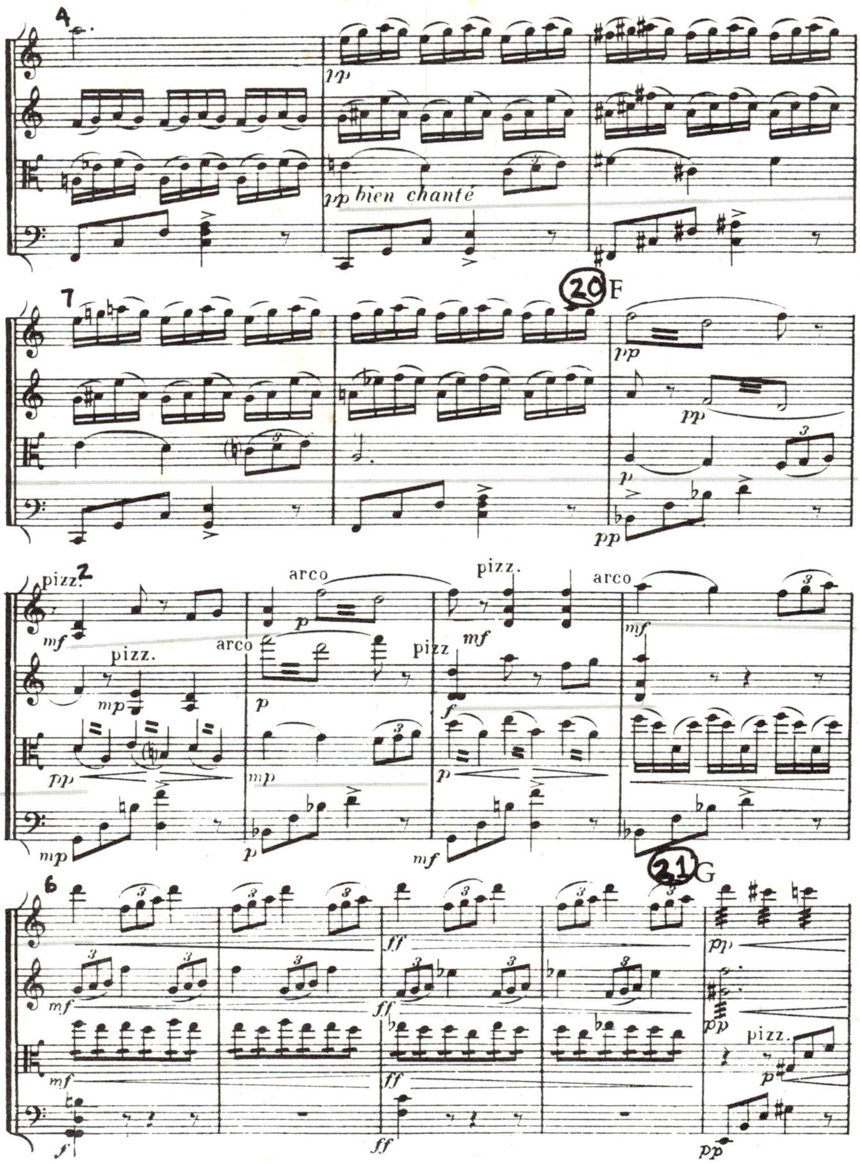
pp bien chanté
20 F
pizz.
arco
pizz.
arco
21 G
pizz.

pizz
pizz.
mettez la Sourdine
mettez la Sourdine
arco
mettez la Sourdine
H Lent (♩ = 46)
arco
arco
porto
p très expressif
mettez. la Sourd.

cédez
a Tempo
mf tres express.
p express.
23 I
4e Corde
mf express.
pizz.
p express.
rall.
arco
a Tempo
pp expressif

9 pressez
pizz.
mf
pp
10 a Tempo
arco
pressez
pizz.
mf
pp
24 J
a Tempo
rall.
a Tempo
pizz.
mp
pizz.
arco
pp un peu marqué
ppp
4
rall.
mf
arco

22 K
25
a Tempo (𝅗𝅥 = 30)
arco
p
expressif
p quazi arpa
pp
pp
2
simile
3
4
rall.

(♩ = 46)
4e Corde
arco
pizz.
ôtez la Sourd.
ôtez la Sourd.
26
Io Tempo
ôtez la Sourd.
ôtez la Sourd.
pizz.
pizz.
pizz.

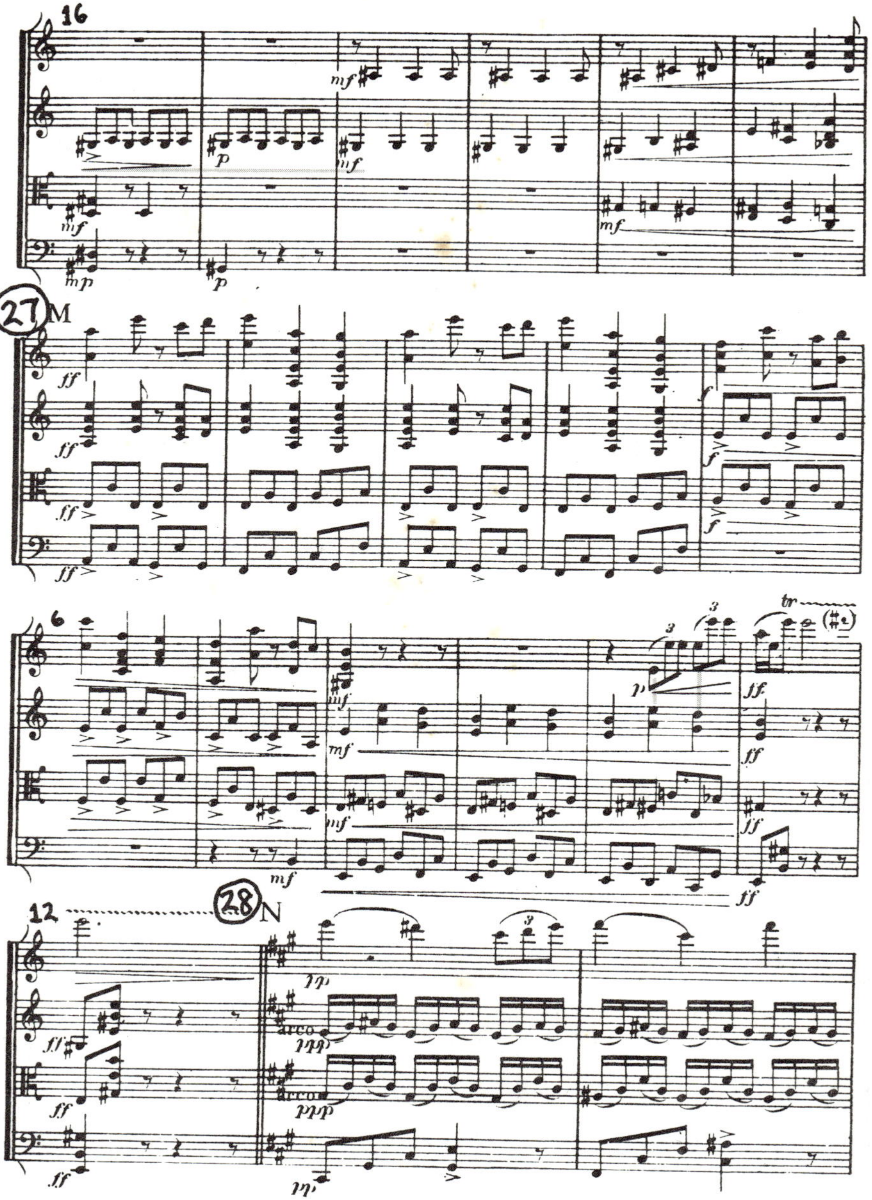
16
27
M
6
tr
12
28
N
arco
arco

III

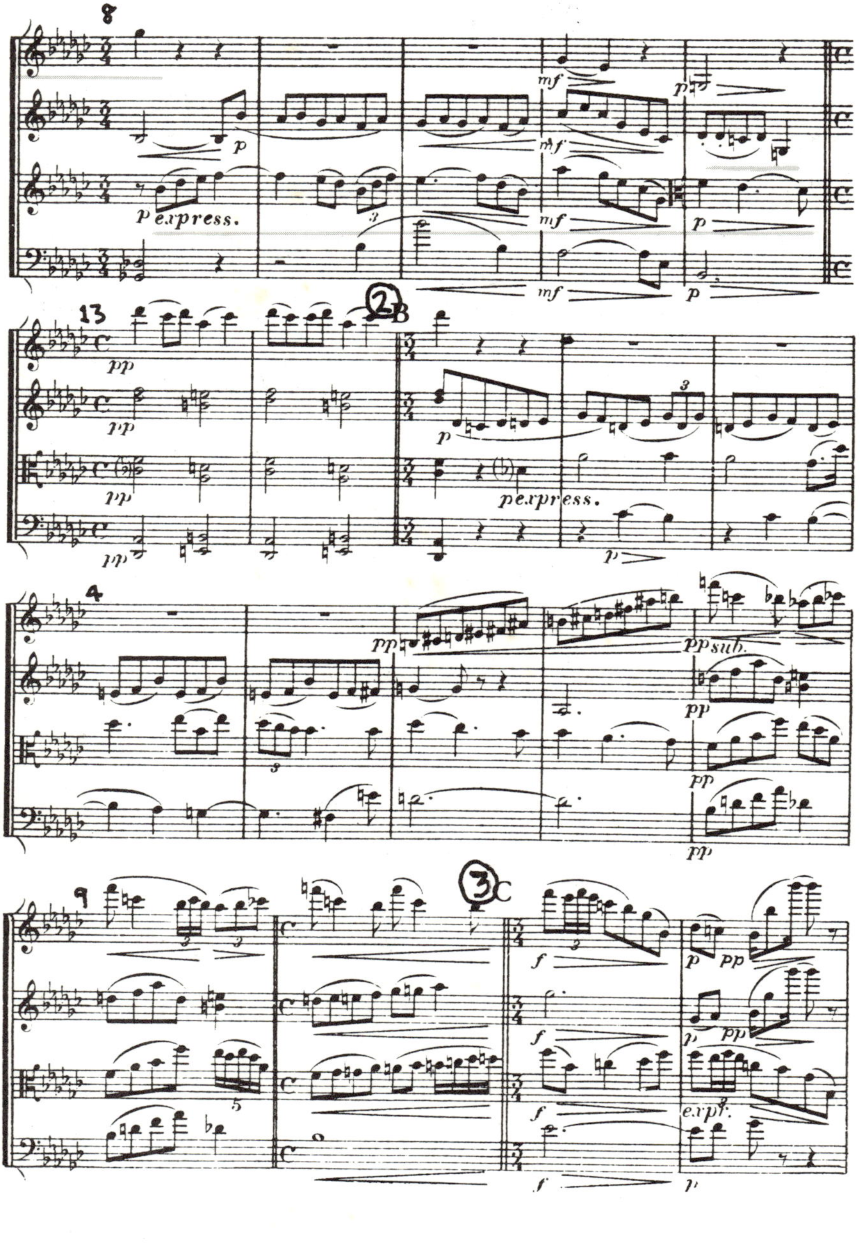
8
p express.
13
2 B
p express.
4
pp sub.
9
3 C
expr.

pp
pp
pp expressif
perdendosi
ppp
Modéré (♩ = 84)
rit.
molto rall.
ôtez la Sourdine
mettez la Sourd.
f
p
fénergique
p express.
a Tempo modto.
Modéré
rit.
rall.
a Tempo
ôtez la Sourdine
mettez la Sourd.
pp

ôtez
ôtez
ôtez
en dehors
Pas trop lent (♩ = 60)
la Sourd.
la Sourd.
la Sourd.
pp
expressif
pizz.
ôtez la Sourdine
arco
mp très expressif
pizz.

Modérément animé ($\boldsymbol{\downarrow}$ = 72)

pressez
6
7
rall.
Modéré
H
ff passionné
passionné
ff
3
cédez
Très calme
f
p
expressif
pp

pizz.
Modéré
arco
mettez la Sourdine
mettez la Sourdine
mettez la
pizz.
rall.
9
I.º Tempo
Sourdine
expressif
arco
mettez la Sourd.
tranquille
10

port.
p expressif
rall.
11 K
pressez
pizz.
arco
rall.
Très lent
rall.
au Mouvt
express.
pp expressif
pizz.
express.
rall.

IRVING FINK (1915-1978), artist graduate of the David Mannes Conservatory in New York, was a concert violinist and founder of many string quartets, a member of the Cleveland Orchestra, and a professional bow-maker. A wrist injury on Okinawa in World War II ended his career as a professional violinist.

CYNTHIA MERRIELL, music education graduate, amateur violinist and free-lance writer, met Irving Fink at a chamber music get-together and worked closely with him to bring this book to fruition. After his death, she assembled the chapters and completed the red-lining of the scores from his notes.

"For me, it is in chamber music and particularly string quartet playing that the greatest moments are to be found. Each player is so integral, the whole so dependent on each of our parts, the public performances so demanding of all our combined leadership qualities, the intimacy imposing such constraints on our sound control, the rewards so immediate and profound, that we become participants in a unique and sublime form of communication. When I learned that Irving wanted to share his concepts of quartet playing, I urged him to do so, offering whatever assistance I could give to the project."

Cynthia Merriell
Los Gatos, California
1977

188

The late Mr. Fink's and Ms. Merriell's amiable collaboration is beautifully symbolized by this picture of them playing string quartet music together at Mr. Fink's house.

Irving Fink   Cynthia Merriell